An Introduction to
Library and
Information
Work

Anne Totterdell

with contributions from
Jane Gill and **Alan Hornsey**

facet publishing

© Anne Totterdell 1998, 2001, 2005

Published by
Facet Publishing
7 Ridgmount Street
London WC1E 7AE

Facet Publishing is wholly owned by CILIP: the Chartered Institute of Library and Information Professionals.

First published 1998 as *The Library and Information Work Primer*
Second edition 2001
This third edition published as *An Introduction to Library and Information Work*, 2005

British Library Cataloguing in Publication Data
A catalogue record for this book is available from the British Library.

ISBN 1-85604-557-9

Typeset in 10/13 Century Schoolbook and MicroSquare by Facet Publishing.
Printed and made in Great Britain by MPG Books Ltd, Bodmin, Cornwall.

Contents

Preface

The publication of *An Introduction to Library and Information Work*, the third edition of *The Library and Information Primer*, first published in 1998, reflects the continuing need for a textbook to replace earlier editions as the standard work for paraprofessional library staff and for the introductory year of professional library and information courses.

This edition, with its additional chapter on the global perspective and particularly on libraries in the developing world, will also be of use to non-UK students and to anyone who, through personal interest or through working in comparable or similar sectors, needs an overview of libraries and their current concerns and practices. We intend it to support the two major qualifications for paraprofessional library staff in the UK, the Information and Library Services National Vocational Qualifications and the City and Guilds 7371 (the Information and Library Services Progression Award Level 3), and to be a support to paraprofessional staff seeking accreditation under the new CILIP Framework of Qualifications (see Chapter 2).

As with previous editions, we hope to provide a comprehensive, accurate and detailed basis for library and information studies as well as an introduction for the interested layman – a basis which is as current and as broad as we can ensure. This breadth and currency is supported by the varying backgrounds of the contributors: Anne Totterdell is from a lecturing and academic context, Alan Hornsey from an IT context, and Jane Gill, who has revised Lyn Pullen's excellent chapter, from a senior library management context.

We must also mention our continuing debt to Colin Harrison, who, with Rosemary Beenham, was a pioneer in the field of textbooks for paraprofessional library staff and who shared the responsibility for the first edition of the present work with Anne Totterdell. Thanks are also due to: Sue Berry (Somerset County Record Office), Jane Fitzgerald (Somerset College of Arts and Technology), Liz Fothergill (Taunton Citizens Advice Bureau), Alfred Fullah (Oxford Citizens Advice Bureau) and Andrew Hopkins (Taunton Tourist Information Bureau).

In all occupations there are pedestrian and boring bits. We hope, however, that readers of this book will pick up the absorbing interest, the variety, the excitement and the fulfilment which are far more characteristic of working within a sector where many different types of people find high levels of job satisfaction. Now, more than ever, great emphasis is placed on the vital importance of information to an efficient society, and of social inclusion and education for life to a contented society, and the role of libraries in achieving progress in these vital areas has never been so crucial.

General introduction

We hope that library and information students, both paraprofessional and professional, in the UK and further afield, will find this book helpful in their studies, and that it will also be of value to anyone interested in the sector.

We feel it is particularly opportune that this edition being published in the same year that the new CILIP Framework of Qualifications is being introduced, as it supports both Level 3 qualifications (NVQ 3 and City and Guilds 7371), which are part of the route for paraprofessional staff towards achieving formal acccreditation. Indeed we feel that this new edition, with its broad yet focused approach, will play its part in supporting library and information staff at all levels seeking progression through the Framework, and will continue to feature in the first year of library degree courses.

We have tried to give this edition a less insular approach and hope that non-UK colleagues who found the first two editions of this book useful will find this third edition to be even more so.

Chapter 8 is a new chapter which we hope will contribute towards a global overview and will also highlight current issues which we feel to be important.

In this edition we have also tried to address the needs of interested lay people working outside the library and information sector but needing an overview of current significant issues in the sector. We are thinking in particular of teachers with library and/or budgeting responsibilities, local government staff and local authority councillors, who need such information to make informed decisions on issues which impinge on the library and information sector.

You will find that we have used examples of library and information units local to us in Chapter 1, because of our familiarity with them. We very much appreciate the input from local library and information unit managers (see Preface).

The library and information sector is an absorbing and stimulating area in which to work, an area that is currently experiencing rapid changes in both perspective and operations. We all need to work or study in an identifiable context and it seems sensible to begin this book with a survey of some of the most significant current issues in the field.

Funding

Undoubtedly, the most pressing concern in most areas of library and information work is that of funding.

Public libraries

For many years, all local government services have had to fight for their share of a limited budget, and public libraries have all too often been the losers in this particular battle despite the undoubted improvement in central government attitudes to, and support for, public libraries since the election of a Labour Government in 1997. It is a paradox that, although libraries undoubtedly figure more prominently in central government policy than they did, being clearly viewed as major players in education for life, social inclusion and the provision of online information, and although there has been greatly increased expenditure on, for example, ICT training for public library staff and prestige new library buildings (in Peckham, Braintree and Brighton), funding remains an issue. To quote *Library and Information Update* of December 2004, discussing the NFER report *Extending the Role of Libraries*, 'Today's public library does far more than "lending and information"; but lack of secure funding threatens to wreck it all' (CILIP, 2004, 10).

There has been a great deal of debate and disagreement as to how library services can best deal with financial hardship – closure of branches, reductions in opening hours, drastic reduction in stock expenditure, replacement of qualified staff with unqualified, flatter management structures, finding outside partnerships and grants, and exploration of various income generation options – but there is general agreement that all too often serious funding problems remain. Until very recently library provision has not figured very prominently in national political agendas, but the picture is encouragingly different at local level, where many a battle to preserve threatened services has been fought and indeed won, and where the letter pages of local newspapers are full of the protests of angry citizens whose local library services have been in the firing line.

Other libraries

The financial situation is also often critical in academic libraries. School libraries and school library services have been particularly vulnerable, with levels of provision falling despite the requirements of the National Curriculum, and some school library services being withdrawn completely. Even special libraries and information units within industrial organizations have not escaped the general financial blight and are all too often regarded as expendable when a down-sizing operation is in progress. The present problems of Aslib (the Association for Information Management; see Chapter 1) spring in part from falling membership.

In short, there is a mismatch between the increasingly acknowledged vital role of the wide range of library and information units in this country, and the ability or willingness to fund that role adequately – a problem that the emerging generation of library and information staff must address. On the plus side, the manner in which dedicated library and information staff strive to maintain service levels in extremely difficult circumstances is greatly to be applauded, as is the increased involvement and support of central government.

What is the library's role?

Another vital current issue is that of role – what are libraries actually for? During the past few years, this focus on the role of libraries has to some extent changed emphasis in a changing political climate

The traditional public library in the UK has been based on four keystones: culture, education, leisure and recreation, and information. Different political viewpoints have in recent years placed varying emphases on these four keystones. Current political thinking and government policy has, with the successful introduction of the People's Network, and the lottery-funded ICT training of library staff, put great emphasis on the information role of libraries, while at the same time promoting the role of libraries as vehicles for lifelong learning information and opportunities, as community facilities (homework clubs and computer clubs) and perhaps most significantly as tools for social inclusion.

Status and pay

The status, pay and image of library staff at all levels across a wide range of library and information units in the UK have always been problematic, and most practitioners in the sector believe that the situation is deteriorating rather than improving. The reasons why librarianship as a profession in Britain has never had the status and salary entitlements enjoyed by librarians in some other countries form an involved and complex area which is not appropriate to this book. It is perhaps sufficient to say that, while 30 years ago librarians and teachers were roughly equivalent in terms of training, status and pay, librarians have fallen considerably behind – a quick glance at the salaries in CILIP's *Library and Information Gazette* will confirm this. There are widespread misconceptions about library staff – very few members of the public or of other professions can distinguish between a graduate chartered librarian and a library assistant. Little has been done for the status of library staff by the recent increased use of volunteers in public libraries.

Image

Public library staff do still have an image and status problem and, in many ways, the problem is even worse for academic library staff, who continue to fight an uphill battle, both at school and college level, for a realistic recognition of the immense contribution they make.

Again, it is not our purpose to address these problems in any depth here, beyond saying that it is becoming increasingly clear that library staff need to add the skills of self-publicizing and political astuteness to their professional expertise and dedication. We are a predominantly female profession and score very highly on commitment and hard work, and possibly less highly on political acumen. This may have to change. It seems particularly incongruous that the sector should continue to have this image problem when we are increasingly supposed to be leading others along the information superhighway, and facilitating the development of an information society

Gender issues

As has been pointed out, librarianship is a predominantly female sector. Over 90% of paraprofessional library staff are women and at professional level 70% of library school entrants are women. This imbalance has had all the effects that one might have expected and clearly impacts on salary, status and training at all levels.

Although in terms of numbers women predominate in the profession, the chances of women reaching top management positions, particularly in public libraries, remain extremely low. We can only touch briefly here on the reasons for the promotion difficulties still experienced by women in our sector:

1   Recent research on women in employment in general has revealed the damaging effects of working part-time and of career breaks for child-care on women's career prospects in today's work-focused society. Our sector has been backward in terms of appropriate working hours, holiday entitlement and part-time and jobshare opportunities to meet the needs of mothers wishing to return to work, let alone in ensuring that the employment prospects of women are not damaged.

2   The restriction of professional training opportunities (with a few valuable exceptions) to full-time education, a constraint introduced in the 1960s and only recently challenged by the introduction of part-time and distance learning options, undoubtedly meant that many able women employees were prevented from reaching their full potential. However the new CILIP Framework of Qualifications (see Chapter 2) is very good news for women in the sector at all levels.

3   The sector has not completely emerged from its sexist past, when training structures and employment policies reflected attitudes that would now be deplored: for example, equal pay for men and women in libraries only came in in the 1950s and there was a lingering prejudice against the employment of married women well into the 1960s. The patronizing elements in early paraprofessional syllabi reflect the fact that nearly all paraprofessionals have been women. We believe that residual sexist attitudes still affect women's promotion prospects in the library and information sector.

Censorship

A number of other current issues will be encountered in the library and information sector, most of which will be touched upon in later chapters. Issues of censorship, for example, have always generated a great deal of controversy within the sector, particularly more recently in the context of political correctness. Currently, too, uncensored material available on the internet has rightly become a major focus for concern. While there is a clear requirement both to operate within the law and to protect the vulnerable, attitudes to material which may appear sexist or racist vary considerably.

The national press has over the past few years had a great deal of amusement at the expense of libraries that pursue the impossible goal of totally neutral and unbiased stock, for example by the removal of all copies of *The Tale of Mrs Tiggy Winkle* from their shelves on the grounds of unacceptable sexual stereotyping (Mrs Tiggy Winkle being a female washerwoman, albeit a hedgehog!) or by censoring collections of nursery rhymes containing 'Baa baa black sheep' to avoid possible offence to ethnic minorities. Although efforts such as these may appear ridiculous to many, we must appreciate the desire to serve communities as a whole without offence, regardless of class, race or gender.

Censoring politically sensitive material is a difficult issue, with libraries going to great lengths to ensure fairness to all viewpoints while keeping within the law. In a democracy it is a clear duty of all libraries to cover the range of political viewpoints, but how can we reconcile this duty with, for example, the incitement to racial hatred contained in the literature of some minority political parties in this country? Which takes priority: the need to contribute to an informed electorate, or the need to avoid the promulgation of racist attitudes? CILIP offers useful guidelines here, indicating that libraries should not stock material if its prime purpose is propagandist.

We also have the problems of sexually sensitive material: for example, case reports on child abuse may be needed for entirely legitimate purposes by researchers in the field, but could be used inappropriately by others. The problems of censorship will increase with wider access to the internet and, doubtless, responsible librarians will continue to try to operate in the best interests of all in this controversial but fascinating area.

Conclusion

This overview of some of the current issues and ethical concerns of the library and information sector will, we hope, indicate that working in this area in whatever capacity at this particular time of change and revaluation is demanding, exciting and interesting, and deserves our best efforts in terms of an informed and professional approach.

Reference

CILIP (2004) Funding is Still an Issue, *Library and Information Update*, **3** (12), December, 10.
   Discusses the NFER report *Extending the Role of Libraries*, commissioned by the Local Government Association and available at www.nfer.ac.uk/research/project_summaries.asp.

1 The functions and structure of the principal types of library and information service within the UK

This chapter will look at the range of library and information units open to the public, concentrating on the UK.

Public libraries

The public library movement in the UK got underway in the mid-19th century in the context of the increasing educational needs of a rapidly developing industrial nation, and of the Victorian philosophy of self-help and self-improvement. In 1845 the Museums Act was passed: some local authorities, Salford for example, used the provisions of this Act to provide books. Following this limited start, the Select Committee on Public Libraries was set up in 1849, leading to the Public Libraries Act of 1850, which allowed the funding of library provision from local rates (a halfpenny rate in local authority areas of more than 10,000 but nothing to be spent on actual books!). There followed a period of initial growth in provision as local authorities adopted the Act.

Early developments in the establishment of public library services were greatly helped by the Scottish industrialist and philanthropist Andrew Carnegie, who gave library buildings to local communities, some of which remain in use today.

The second half of the 19th century saw the establishment of many of the major UK public libraries: Westminster Public Library in 1857, Birmingham Public Library in 1860, the Mitchell Reference Library, Glasgow, in 1874, Edinburgh Public Library in 1890 and the John Rylands Library, Manchester, in 1899. A number of library acts were also passed in this period, in 1855 (which allowed the product of a penny rate in local authority areas of more than 5000 to be spent on libraries and, for the first time, on books), 1887, 1892, 1893 and 1908. In 1919 a Public Libraries Act abolished the penny rate provision and, importantly, empowered county councils to establish library services for the first time.

County library provision got off to rather a slow start. The 1919 Act was permissive and emphasis, rather misguidedly, was placed primarily on low cost provision. It was some time before the image of boxes of books in village schools and halls, looked after by volunteers – the inevitable result of this approach – was superseded. The pioneering county librarians of the first half of the 20th century developed admirable services despite severe financial restrictions, responding successfully to the increased demand of the war years and the immediate post-war period: their reward came in the 1960s with an impressive building programme and with the 1964 Public Libraries and Museums Act.

This Act replaced earlier legislation and is still the current Act. It requires the Secretary of State for Education and Science to control the comprehensive and efficient library service provided for by the Act, which also established advisory councils and made the provision of library services mandatory. This period saw the taking over by larger library authorities such as county councils or metropolitan borough councils of libraries operated by small local authorities, on the grounds that small authorities could not provide library services of an acceptable standard. Reorganization along these lines in order to establish and maintain adequate standards in library provision had been recommended in two major reports produced in the period leading up to the Act, the *McColvin Report* (1942) and the *Roberts Report* (1959). The Local Government Act of 1972 finally enshrined this policy in law.

Public libraries have come a long way in the last century and a half, going through periods of expansion and attrition, and constantly adapting to the needs of the user in terms of developing and changing services.

Statistics available at the time of writing (Library and Information Statistics Unit, 2004) show that book loans are down slightly (4.2%) but visits to public libraries are up by 1.5%, the latter probably indicating the success of the People's Network, an initiative linking England's libraries to the internet and online services. Levels of satisfaction with library services remain high, although there has been a backlash recently in the popular press against the replacement of book stocks with computers, indicating the continuing popularity of the booklending aspect of library services.

Structure and finance

A county library system is used here as an example of public library provision. Although there is no standardized structure for public library provision, which is spread across previously existing counties, metropolitan and London boroughs, and new unitary authorities set up in the mid-1990s, most county libraries have a similar structure to this example:

- an administrative headquarters, often not open to the public, where the main administrative procedures of the service – financial management, personnel management, book selection, ordering, processing, classification and cataloguing, for example – are carried out centrally
- full-time and part-time branches, mobile and travelling libraries and special libraries, such as local history collections and music and drama libraries.

Staffing of county libraries is headed up by a county or chief librarian, who is a local government chief officer and whose post may also encompass other areas (arts or culture for example). S/he may have a deputy or, in these days of flatter management structures, be supported by a team of assistant county librarians, who may have special subject responsibilities such as young people's services, bibliographic services or reference services. Within the county service there may be geographical divisions, each headed by a divisional or area librarian, often with a deputy, while at branch level senior or branch librarians run the service, with their own supporting infrastructure of specialist children's and reference staff and librarians with responsibility for the day-to-day running of stock, requests and enquiry services. All of these are normally chartered or qualified librarians. Supporting the general public services are paraprofessional and support staff.

County libraries are financed via the local authority, but may also generate income by, for example, charging for services other than book loans: video and cassette loans, online searches, fax and photocopying services, selling their own publications, hiring out premises for concerts or meetings, fines and selling unwanted stock.

The user population

A public library is responsible for meeting the needs of everyone living in its catchment area in terms of education, information, culture, leisure and recreation. Currently, public library stock and its issue reflects predominantly the leisure and recreation aspects of the library role, in that fiction forms the major proportion of each. However, we are seeing increasing emphasis on the information role, with vastly increased use of the internet. More users of public libraries now use the internet than read newspapers.

The needs of special client groups must also be effectively met. Most county library services serve the needs of, for example, prisoners within their area, by providing professional support to prison library staff as well as periodically changed book collections. The needs of the housebound reader can also be met in a similar way. Most public libraries are acutely aware of the needs of clients with special problems, and provide wheelchair access, and special facilities for vision- or hearing-impaired users. Kent Arts and Libraries, for example, issues leaflets listing such services. Deaf people are offered induction loops in major libraries, close-captioned videos minicoms, collections of books about deafness and hearing loss for adults and children, and staff who are trained in deaf-awareness and basic sign-language skills. Exeter Central Library is an admirable example of a public library that has taken immense trouble to meet the needs of disadvantaged users, providing, for example, talking newspapers, wheelchair hoists and clear directional signs (including clearly marked carpets for visually impaired users). Most public libraries stock large-print books and lend audio cassettes free to visually-impaired users. There have been significant initiatives in recent years to cater to the needs of minorities such as refugees and asylum seekers, and the gypsy and traveller communities (see Chapter 7).

Public library staff are well aware of how important it is to meet the needs of children, not only to ensure that they grow to be enthusiastic library users but also because, as recent library initiatives such as 'Babies Need Books' have shown, early exposure to the world of books is highly beneficial to the social as well as the educational development of young children. A bright and spacious children's area, specialist staff, story times, competitions, holiday activities, author visits, videos, badges and playgroup and school visits have become the norm in public libraries, to the great benefit of the community.

Public libraries situated in areas where there are many local industries, or in large commercial centres, will normally offer also appropriate support to this special client group.

Public libraries normally restrict their lending to people living or working in their catchment area. When a reader joins the library, having demonstrated eligibility, a reader ticket is given which allows a specified number of loans. On the other hand, the reference stock of a public library, which will vary in comprehensiveness according to the size of the library – some counties concentrate their reference function in one main county reference library – may be used by anyone. It will consist of printed and electronic reference sources and will increasingly include access to the internet, due to the establishment of the People's Network.

Public libraries need to be at the heart of their communities: information in the form of files of local newspapers and lists of local organizations, as well as internet access, exhibition space for such organizations, the use of library premises for local events and the involvement of library staff in community activities, all emphasize the importance of this specific function. The present government sees public libraries as having a particularly significant role in social inclusion measures (see Chapter 7).

Archive services

Also available to the public are central and local government archives. Central government archives are held in the Public Record Office, while local government archives are held in county record offices or, more rarely, in district record offices. The material held in record offices is distinct from that held in local history libraries in that:

- it is not usually authored
- it is primary source material rather than secondary source material, consisting of a variety of documents which have been described as the 'sediments of administration'
- it is material covering the last 800 years, relevant to the locality but no longer required for its original purposes.

Security is vital, because much of the material is totally irreplaceable: the loan of original material is therefore not allowed. The nature of the material also means that specialist help is normally required if the user is to make full use of the source.

Archivists' professional training is different from that of librarians and consists of a one-year postgraduate course, currently offered at four universities. The professional body is the Society of Archivists, which accredits the postgraduate courses and also offers its own in-service training. There is no specific qualification for paraprofessional archive staff, but most paraprofessional record office staff receive appropriate in-service training. Status and salary rates are similar to those of library staff.

Record offices are funded by local government and have been affected in some areas by local government reorganization, which can mean that a record office may serve an entire county but be funded by only part of it. For example, in 1974, when the county of Avon was created, the Somerset County Record Office continued to serve the original county, including Avon, while receiving no Avon funding. Similar anomalies arose from another more recent round of reorganization.

We will take as a case study the Somerset County Record Office at Taunton. Here, 8500 user visits are handled by the County Archivist and five other professionally qualified archivists, with 5.5 paraprofessional staff who deal with reception, administration and searchroom supervision and support. The paraprofessional staff are the first line of contact with enquirers, and call in a member of the professional staff only if they feel it necessary. There are also specialist staff dealing with documents, conservation, records management and reprographics, and 1.5 researchers whose services are charged for.

In a typical year, 60% of the enquiries at Somerset County Record Office concern genealogy, 10% history of houses, 6% history of a locality (for local history authors) and 4% relate to legal or administrative concerns (for example, rights of way). Out of the total number of enquiries, 6% are from people in full-time education. Use by individuals researching for themselves is free, but charges are made for supplying copies of original material, and for the services of researchers.

Some of the most frequently used material at the Somerset County Record Office, for example many of the parish registers, is on microfilm, and archivists regularly visit local libraries with microfilmed material. Many of the records are deposited or lent by other local authorities, by local businesses and by local churches.

The Record Office receives enquiries in person and by letter, fax or telephone, and also via e-mail through the Somerset County Council website on the internet, particularly from the USA and Australia.

The majority of the office's catalogues went online in August 2003. This has led to an increase in the number of enquiries received by e-mail: 2904 e-mail, 1920 postal and 12,891 telephone enquiries were received in the financial year 2003–4.

Academic libraries
University libraries

University libraries range from the very largest, such as the Bodleian at Oxford and the University Library at Cambridge, which are virtually national libraries in that they are entitled to receive materials free of charge under the Legal Deposit system (which requires publishers to deposit all new publications free of charge to The British Library), to much smaller collections similar to those in colleges of further education. The interests of university libraries are represented by the Standing Conference of National and University Libraries (SCONUL), which was founded in 1950.

The services and stock of a university library reflect the courses offered and the type and amount of research undertaken by the institution. The client group will consist of undergraduate students, graduate and research students and university staff, all of whose needs differ and must be met. There must be reference and lending material at appropriate levels, a considerable proportion of which may be serial publications, reports and learned journals. There may be the theses of previous students. Many university libraries, particularly the older institutions, have built up special collections of manuscripts and archive material, some of which are of international significance. There must be appropriate audiovisual material, online public access catalogues (OPACs), computing facilities, interlending facilities, study spaces, appropriate IT services such as online facilities (all UK universities are connected to JANET, the Joint Academic Network), a networked CD-ROM system and access to the internet, information and enquiry services, desktop publishing (DTP), fax and photocopying facilities and specialist subject-based support. Increasingly, as university libraries open for longer hours to reflect student need, self-issuing systems are becoming common.

The vogue in higher and further education is currently for converged services, that is, the bringing together of all library, computing and audiovisual services, and this may well be evident.

University library and information staff may be expected to have subject as well as library qualifications. Staffing structures are variable: reporting to a university librarian there may be faculty librarians and/or deputy or subject librarians, supported by paraprofessional and support staff.

Increasingly, online facilities are being developed, with networked services and e-learning becoming the norm, and with periodical resources frequently available mainly through online subscriptions. Zoe Toft recently wrote about the fact that, increasingly, academics are incorporating aspects of e-learning into their syllabi, using virtual learning environments (Toft, 2004, 42–3).

Library facilities at universities may be centralized or there may be multiple sites at individual colleges and subject-based libraries. These facilities are normally open for very long hours, including evenings and weekends (even occasionally all night) in order to meet the needs of their users. Universities, and therefore their libraries, are funded by the Higher Education Funding Council.

College libraries

The libraries of colleges of further and/or higher education may vary considerably in terms of structure, stock and services. They may be autonomous, part of a department or faculty, or part of central college services.

Libraries in colleges are often called learning resource centres, to emphasize the fact that they are no longer entirely book-based. If a college has a policy of convergence, its learning resource centre may include a combination of book, serial, audiovisual, IT, computing, careers, open learning and reprographics resources. As with university libraries, the way forward seems to lie in the development of online resources (see above).

The client group is broader than that of a university library in that it encompasses, as well as college staff, a wider range of students. Further education colleges now offer full support to students with learning difficulties and disabilities, and to postgraduates, as well as to their traditional clientele. The stock and services must reflect the needs of all. Sometimes lending facilities are offered to members of other academic institutions or members of the general public. Lending stock may consist of books, periodicals, slides, cassettes and videos, and must both support the curricula and educate in the broader sense. The fiction stock is normally small, but there will be a wide range of periodicals, both current and retrospective, and a substantial reference stock, both printed and electronic.

There will be OPAC provision, study spaces, interlibrary loans, fax, photocopying and DTP facilities, internet access, an enquiry service and the provision of induction sessions and training in information retrieval and research skills, sometimes subject-based. It has been found that the latter are particularly useful when taught by library staff, timetabled and assessed. In recent years, the balance of resources has been changing, with far more emphasis being placed on electronic sources.

Staffing in the college libraries/learning resource centres is variable. They may be headed by a chief librarian (often called a director of learning resources), sometimes with head of department status. He/she will be chartered and may have teaching or other professional qualifications. There will normally be a team of professionally qualified librarians, some with teaching or other qualifications and/or subject expertise, to head the various sections, and they will be supported by paraprofessional library staff, clerical staff and technical staff.

Since incorporation, when further education colleges left local authority control and became independent businesses, colleges have been responsible for managing their own budgets, which are allocated to them through the newly created Learning and Skills Councils. The governors and principal of each have ultimate responsibility, but the librarian would normally be allocated a budget, either directly or through a department, and have responsibility for managing expenditure.

Integrated learning centres

Many further education colleges are creating integrated learning centres (ILCs). These are centres that have developed from the traditional library and may have a range of titles, such as learning centre or resources centre.

At the Somerset College of Arts and Technology, purpose-built ILCs have been developed to support the curriculum needs of the students. The five ILCs at this college support particular curriculum areas and aim to integrate fully the use of printed and electronic resources into the college curriculum. Each ILC contains subject-specific printed and electronic resources, PCs, scanners, photocopiers and audiovisual resources such as televisions and interactive whiteboards. They also include teaching rooms, study rooms, meeting rooms and individual and group work areas. More significantly, the ILC team includes practitioners who complement the professional and paraprofessional librarians. These staff may include subject-specialist lecturers, IT support staff, dyslexia, literacy and numeracy specialists and learning support staff (who may offer personal and financial guidance).

The ILC teams develop a co-ordinated approach to support students in both their curriculum and wider needs. The ILC team works with the lecturers to ensure the provision of appropriate and up-to-date resources in a range of formats. They also develop resources to support the curriculum and avoid duplication of materials. Anatomy and physiology are taught across a range of disciplines from sport to beauty therapy, and so one ILC team has developed a specialist software package in partnership with lecturers to meet these curriculum needs.

Teaching sessions are also delivered in the ILC to maximize the use of resources and staff expertise. Across the teams, staff are encouraged to develop multiple skills. IT staff may gain paraprofessional library qualifications, library staff may gain IT qualifications, and professional librarians are encouraged to study for teaching qualifications.

School libraries

Since the advent of the National Curriculum with its emphasis on resource-based learning, the importance of the services of a school library/resource centre should be clear to all concerned. Unfortunately, this is one of the areas within the library and information sector that has been hit particularly hard by the current funding crisis, and it would be true to say that, in terms of expenditure, we have witnessed a decline over the last few years, with expenditure on books per pupil decreasing annually, making it increasingly difficult for schools to meet the national standards. School library services are also in decline.

Since the introduction of local management of schools, which means that the head and the governors of each state primary and secondary school have control over their own budgets, and thus decide for themselves whether or not to buy into the local school library resources service and how much to spend on books, many difficult decisions have had to be made. All too often those decisions have adversely affected the school library. Libraries in the private school sector also vary a great deal but it would be true to say that often their funding is not such a problem.

School libraries vary a great deal in what they include: they may be entirely book-based, or they may encompass reprographics, information technology or a careers library. Staffing is also variable. A senior member of the management or teaching staff (for example the Head of English) may have ultimate management responsibility. Funding problems have meant that it is increasingly rare for a school library to be professionally staffed: it is far more likely that the library is run on a day-to-day basis by a library assistant, poorly paid and not professionally qualified but expected to carry out a range of professional duties with the support of the school library resource service if one still operates locally. In some school libraries there is a teacher-librarian, although the appropriate qualification, the Teacher-

Librarian's Certificate, no longer exists. Voluntary help is also significant, particularly in primary school libraries where parents are often very much involved. School library staff encounter problems with isolation and poor status, but are admirably supported by the School Library Association and by the School Libraries Group of CILIP, although the latter tends to concentrate on professional school library staff.

School libraries and resource centres are there to support the staff and pupils of the school, although occasionally you can find a dual purpose library which serves both the school and the local community. The stock of a school library needs to relate very specifically to the needs of the National Curriculum. It will normally consist of a general reference collection, a lending stock that supports the curriculum, a stock of creative literature appropriate to the age range of the pupils, magazines, topic packs, non-printed materials such as slides, videos, cassettes and films, and electronic sources such as CD-ROMs. Increasingly there will be access to the internet. Study spaces are normally available. Photocopying, fax and DTP facilities are also possible. It is particularly important in school libraries that there should be timetabled and assessed induction and information retrieval sessions taught by library staff as information specialists, as part of an ongoing developmental programme. In recent years, school library staff have been able to benefit from the government's New Opportunities funded ICT training.

School library services

Until recently, school library services – supporting state school libraries in a wide range of areas, including professional advice, central purchasing, classification and cataloguing, permanent, long-term or short-term collections, project provision, book selection, planning, library design and computerization – were funded by the local education authority and administered by the public library services, using teams headed by qualified and experienced library staff. This professional support became invaluable as the number of school libraries with qualified staff became fewer. Since the introduction of local management of schools, headteachers can choose whether or not to buy into their local school library service, and these services will survive only if sufficient schools (which can now include non-state schools) choose to do so. The current situation remains problematic, with many school library services closing or under threat of closure, and expenditure by school library services on books and services falling. Many librarians regard developments in this area as a matter of the gravest concern, particularly when viewed in the context of the demands of the National Curriculum and current concerns about educational standards, as well as falling expenditure on material in public libraries for children. It is especially unfortunate in view of the extremely high quality of the support offered by school library services.

Special libraries

Special libraries and information units, now often called workplace libraries, cover a wide range of operations, and include those in government departments (for example, the Charity Commission in Taunton), commercial and industrial organizations (for example, multinational companies such as ICI), medical organizations (for example, hospital trusts and teaching hospitals) and research and professional associations (for example, CILIP). They also include libraries and information units serving the media (for example, the Hulton Picture Library).

Special librarianship and information work is supported by two professional bodies: CILIP, which was formed by the amalgamation of the Library Association and the Institute of Information Scientists, and Aslib, which is currently experiencing some difficulties, having gone into voluntary liquidation in December 2004 and emerging as a private company in February 2005. 'Aslib's long-term viability will depend on whether members decide to stay, whether they see Aslib as value for money, and whether the organisation can continue to provide the services they require' (Privatisation Raises Concerns, 2005, 3).

The most significant characteristics of a special library or information service are its limited client group (for example, the library of a professional association or a commercial company serves only members of that association or company and is not available to the general public) and its limited subject coverage, which would normally cover only subjects connected with the functions of the parent organization (for example, the library of a hospital trust or a teaching hospital would consist largely of medical material). In other words, the main purpose of a special library is to enable the staff of the parent organization to carry out their duties more effectively, thus saving time and, particularly in the case of the libraries in commercial organizations, money for the parent body. These aims mean that the emphases of special librarianship differ somewhat from those of the public and academic libraries we have already discussed.

The paramount necessity for information in a special library or information unit to be up-to-date means that the stock will contain a very large proportion of serial publications, reports and papers. There may also be electronic reference sources, online facilities and appropriate audio-visual material.

Staff are likely to have an information science background, with expertise in the retrieval, handling and dissemination of information, usually, though not always, of a scientific or technical nature. They may well also have an appropriate subject background. They need to be able to help their clientèle keep up-to-date with current developments in their fields, by means of current awareness bulletins or automated selective dissemination of information (SDI) systems. The use of current awareness bulletins or SDI ensures that members of the organization are kept informed of all appropriate publications in their field through the expertise of the librarian/information scientist, thus saving time and money for the parent organization, while the librarian has the satisfaction of ensuring that the stock of the library or information unit is fully exploited. Unlike the operations of public and academic libraries, those of a special library or information unit are often characterized by the need for commercial confidentiality.

Information centres

A variety of information units offer various types of information to the public. Some often operate within libraries on a regular basis, for example legal surgeries or social services information sessions. The best known information centres in the UK are, however, Tourist Information Centres (TICs) and Citizens Advice Bureaux (CABs), both of which operate nationally. We must also note the establishment of the medical helpline NHS Direct.

Tourist Information Centres

There are currently over 600 TICs in the UK, some attached to libraries, some not. Some are open all the year round while some operate seasonally. They offer a range of services to both local residents and visitors. Local residents may obtain information on a very wide range of holiday destinations throughout the UK, while information on local amenities is available to tourists. Booking services for accommodation, theatre tickets and coach travel may be available.

The structure, staffing and funding of TICs may vary: as a case study, we will take the TIC in Taunton, Somerset, which operates from premises attached to the public library. Various bodies are involved in its provision of tourist information: Visit Britain contributes in terms of guidelines and strategies. The main support, however, comes from Taunton Deane Borough Council which pays the running costs of the centre, including rent to the County Library Department for its accommodation.

In Taunton, the TIC staff (two full-time and four part-time assistants) is responsible to the District Council Tourism Officer. Staff qualifications vary. It is likely in the future that TIC managers will need to have degrees in travel and tourism. TIC assistants are expected to have been educated to GCSE standard and where possible to have expertise in at least one foreign language.

The Taunton TIC deals with about 120,000 enquiries each year, using a wide range of leaflets and publications, some of which are free. The material on offer may have been produced by Visit Britain, local councils or commercial publishers. TICs increasingly use appropriate information technology, with the internet a major source of research material. Although many of the services offered by TICs across the UK are free, there is an increasing emphasis on income generation and the desirability of operating as a business rather than as a service as a means of survival. As public resources become reduced the future of tourist offices becomes ever more vulnerable.

Citizens Advice Bureaux

Probably the best known information units in the UK are the Citizens Advice Bureaux, of which there are over 900 with a total staff of more than 20,000, offering free, impartial and confidential advice on a range of legal, social and consumer issues. The six major areas in which information and advice are given are debt, welfare rights, consumer issues, housing, employment and relationship breakdown. Founded in 1939, CAB aims and principles are:

> to ensure that individuals do not suffer through lack of knowledge of their rights and responsibilities or of the services available to them or through an inability to express their needs effectively and equally to exercise a responsible influence on the development of social policies and services, both locally and nationally.   (CAB introductory pack)

There are trustees with overall legal and financial governance, paid managerial staff and highly trained volunteer advisers as well as volunteer receptionists, administrators and IT specialists. The adviser training takes around nine hours per week for six months and once on the advice rota advisers continue with a weekly commitment of around nine hours. All CAB belong to the National Association (formerly NACAB and now known as Citizens Advice), which is responsible for standards and policies and the compulsory basic training of volunteers. Citizens Advice reviews the efficiency and quality of advice of the individual bureaux by means of audit on a three-year basis. Each bureau is independent, self-governing and autonomous.

Expert advice and information is given on all topics and, in addition, many CAB represent clients at social security appeals and employment tribunals, also acting as mediator between clients and third parties when appropriate.

Taunton CAB, as a case study, like many other bureaux relies heavily on local government funding (through county and district councils) although there is some central funding administered through Citizens Advice (mainly for training), and 5% of its funding is self-generated (for example, from the parish councils and from voluntary contributions). Taunton CAB has 36 volunteer advisers, 12 volunteer support workers and 14 volunteer receptionists. There is one full-time salaried manager, three other management staff, a part-time money advice and welfare benefits officer and a clerical worker. Project work currently includes staff working for Sure Start Taunton, an adviser working in the county court every day, a mental health outreach worker and an anti-poverty and home-visit adviser. Legal Help (formerly Legal Aid) is available for debt advice for clients who have little or no income. Outreach services are provided once a week at Wellington, Wiveliscombe and other centres around Taunton.

Staff are kept completely up to date via the comprehensive Citizens Advice electronic information system, which is available to staff only. Clients can access a public website www.adviceguide.org.uk which offers advice on frequently asked questions in six different languages.

Citizens Advice Bureaux face constant challenges because of increasing demand, particularly in the area of debt and benefits. In addition, the budgeting problems of local government often mean that CAB managers have to give more time to fund-raising than is ideal. However, there can be no doubt about the vital role Citizens Advice Bureaux play in a democracy – both in their support of the individual citizen and in their influence on social policy.

Typical queries would cover income support, debt and how to avoid bailiffs, unfair dismissal from work, child support, how to apply for disability living allowance, asylum and consumer problems.

National libraries

In the developed world it is usual for countries to have established national libraries – libraries that are government funded and that serve the nation as a whole. National libraries have a prestige role in terms of their contents and of the buildings that house them. For example, in Paris the Bibliothèque Nationale has moved its 12 million books to the four glass towers of the new Bibliothèque François Mitterand, a £1 billion project which took over eight years to complete and which accommodates 10,000 readers for six days a week; in the UK, the building at St Pancras, which was a long time in construction and extremely costly, houses the vast collections of the British Library; and in the USA the Library of Congress functions as a national library although it is not one officially.

National libraries as irreplaceable deposits of national culture can be very vulnerable. The Serbs destroyed most of the collection of the National Library of Bosnia in Sarajevo in 1992, and the Romanian National Library was destroyed in the revolution against Ceausescu in 1990. Irreparable damage was done to the libraries of Iraq during the recent conflict.

National libraries may have a variety of functions: UNESCO has worked to standardize these functions into three categories: main, desirable and possible. The five main, or essential, functions are:

- to collect and conserve the national literature, aiming at complete coverage
- to produce a current national bibliography
- to operate a lending service
- to act as a national bibliographic information service
- to publish and/or support the production of specialist bibliographies.

Desirable functions include:

- acting as a centre for research and development in library and information work
- providing education and training in library and information work

* acting as a planning centre for the nation's libraries.

Possible functions include:

* acting as a centre for the exchange of material between libraries
* providing specialized library services to the country's governing body
* acting as a book museum.

The national libraries of the world vary as to which of these possible functions they concentrate on fulfilling.

The British Library (www.bl.uk)

For the purposes of this section we will concentrate on the UK's national library (its document supply operations are discussed in Chapter 3), which is the national library of the UK, and one of the greatest libraries in the world.

The British Library came into being in 1973, following the Dainton Report and the British Library Act of 1972. It amalgamated the former British Museum Library, the National Central Library, the National Lending Library for Science and Technology and the British National Bibliography. Its stated aims were to act as a 'national centre for reference, study, bibliographical and other information services' to support 'in particular, institutions of education and learning and libraries and information centres in industry'. Its current publicity describes it as 'the world's leading resource for scholarship, research and innovation'. To quote from its current website, 'our vision is to make the world's intellectual, scientific and cultural heritage accessible, and to bring the collections of the British Library to everyone – at work, school, college or home'.

The first services at the new purpose-built premises at St Pancras opened in November 1997. British Library operations are concentrated on two sites – St Pancras, which will house most of the general and specialist collections now scattered over various London sites, and the British Library Document Supply Centre at Boston Spa, which will concentrate on the Library's interlending role (see Chapter 3). A few collections such as the Newspaper Library have not moved to St Pancras.

The emphasis of the functions concentrated on the St Pancras site is on the individual user, rather than on libraries, as is the case with BLDSC at Boston Spa. The opening of the new building coincided with the introduction of the British Library online catalogue and the automated book request system: there are 86 computer terminals for users to search for and order the material they require. Material will then be speedily delivered to the appropriate reading room from the stacks, provided it is available.

Over the last few years we have seen the development of the British Library Integrated Catalogue online. Previously separate catalogues as listed below, are now included:

General printed books pre-1975
Humanities and social sciences post 1975
Humanities and social sciences open access reference books
Science technology and business
Document supply books
Document supply serials
Document supply conferences
Asia Pacific and Africa collections
Cartographic
Newspapers
Printed music

Other specialist catalogues such as the Sound Archives catalogue and the Images Collection remain outside the integrated catalogue

The most recent statistics tell us that the collection includes 150 million items, in most known languages, and that 3 million new items are incorporated every year. There is on-site space for over 1200 readers, and over 16,000 people use the collections each day. Each year, six million searches are generated by the British Library integrated catalogue (http://catalogue.bl.uk).

Library and information staff should also be aware of the Information Sciences collection held by the British Library and accessible at the Humanities Department, Second Floor, at the British Library building at St Pancras.

The British Library also holds 38 million patents.

Professional bodies

A number of professional bodies, some national and some international, support and represent people working in the library and information sector. The best known of these is CILIP: the Chartered Institute of Library and Information Professionals, which was formed by an amalgamation of the Library Association and the Institute of Information Scientists in 2002.

CILIP: the Chartered Institute of Library and Information Professionals

The Library Association was founded in 1877 following the first International Conference of Librarians in London. Its initial stated aims were the regulation of the profession (it must be remembered that librarianship in the modern sense is a relatively new profession), the promotion of better management and administration of libraries, the encouragement of bibliographical study and research and the interchange of information about libraries. The Library Association received its Royal Charter in 1898. A supplemental Royal Charter was granted in 1986.

CILIP: the Chartered Institute of Library and Information Professionals was formed from the unification of The Library Association and the Institute of Information Scientists in April 2002, and a Royal Charter was granted for the new body.

The current role of CILIP may be summarized as follows:

- It represents and acts as the professional body for library and information sector staff.
- It looks carefully at any proposed legislation that may affect library provision.
- It promotes legislation that may improve library provision.
- It promotes the maintenance of appropriate library and information services provision and their better management.
- It promotes the improvement of the training, education and status of library personnel.
- It maintains a register of Chartered members qualified to practise as professional librarians and information personnel.
- It promotes relevant study and research and the effective dissemination of the results of these and indeed of all appropriate information of interest to its members.
- It works with comparable organizations overseas.
- It provides a range of services to its members.

CILIP covers a very wide range of sectors of activity through its special interest groups. Members are entitled to join two such groups free and may join further groups for a small fee. The current list of groups is as follows: Branch and Mobile Libraries; Career Development (formerly the Association of Assistant Librarians); Cataloguing and Indexing; Colleges of Further and Higher Education; Community Services; Diversity; Education Librarians; Government Libraries; Health Libraries; Industrial and Commercial Libraries; Information Services; International; Library History; Library and Information Research; Local Studies; Multimedia Information and Technology; Patent and Trademark; Personnel, Training and Education; Prison Libraries; Public Libraries; Publicity and Public Relations; Rare Books; School Libraries; UKeIG (the UK e-Information Group); University College and Research; and Youth Libraries. There is also an Affiliated Members National Committee and a Retired Members' Guild. Typically, the groups promote local meetings and national conferences as well as producing newsletters. They play an extremely useful role in supporting personnel in specific areas and encouraging the interchange of expertise and experience.

CILIP has its headquarters in London, and the whole of the UK is covered by its 12 branches. Activities are organized both by the special interest groups and centrally, and in addition the branches organize a range of activities such as seminars and training events at a local level, and issue their own branch newsletters. Typically, such events might cover issues of current concern, such as local government reorganization, copyright or European information, but could also deal with, for example, the reading needs of reluctant readers, or recent developments in library technology (see www.cilip.org.uk).

The School Library Association

This is a good example of an organization set up and developed to support library staff in one particular sector. Founded in 1937 to promote and support the development of libraries in schools, the SLA is an independent organization and registered charity, membership of which depends solely on the payment of an annual subscription. There are currently about 3000 members. Its main aims are to support and encourage school libraries, to raise awareness and promote good practice through training (there is a wide range of local and national training initiatives) and a publications programme (which includes the quarterly *School Librarian* and a range of bulletins, leaflets and newsletters) and to draw attention to and campaign for appropriate school library provision (see www.sla.org.uk).

Aslib (The Association for Information Management)

Aslib is an example of an organization with a slightly different emphasis. It offers support to special library staff and information scientists. It was founded in 1924 with the aim of assisting companies and other organizations to manage their information. The subtitle Association for Information Management was added in 1983. Its 2000 members (largely corporate rather than individual) include commercial and industrial organizations, academic institutions and government bodies. Aslib has a strong publications programme (the monthly *Aslib Information* and the quarterly *Journal of Documentation*) as well as an extensive training and advisory programme. However, at the time of writing, Aslib is experiencing some problems. Due largely to financial problems, it went into voluntary liquidation in December 2004, and emerged as a private company in February 2005 (see www.aslib.co.uk).

ARLIS (The Art Libraries Society)

ARLIS is an example of an organization set up to support library staff in one subject area, in this case that of art and design. It was set up in 1969 specifically to promote art librarianship, and to facilitate the exchange of expertise and information between its members. ARLIS holds annual conferences and has a lively publications programme, which includes the quarterly *Art Libraries Journal* (see www.arlis.org.uk).

International organizations

The above are all national organizations, though they may well have links with their counterparts in other countries (for example, ARLIS is affiliated to its American counterpart). The best known international organization is the International Federation of Library Associations and Institutions. Founded in 1927, and with its headquarters in the Netherlands, IFLA now has members from over 130 countries. It is a prestigious organization, with representation on or consultative arrangements with a number of international bodies. Its objectives are comprehensive, focusing on worldwide co-operation and research, education and the development of international guidelines for a wide range of library activities. It operates a range of core programmes to work towards these objectives: for example, the Advancement of Librarianship in the Third World (ALP), and Universal Bibliographic Control and International MAchine Readable Cataloguing, or MARC (UBCIM). IFLA's complex organization into 31 sections and 10 round tables ensures that all aspects of the international library and information world are represented. Its publications include the quarterly *IFLA Journal* and the annual *IFLA Directory* (see www.ifla.org).

References

Dainton, F. (1969) Great Britain, Department for Education and Science, *Report of the National Libraries Committee*, London, HMSO (the Dainton Report).

Library and Information Statistics Unit (2004) *LISU Annual Library Statistics 2004, featuring Trend Analysis of UK Public & Academic Libraries 1993-2003*, Loughborough, LISU.

McColvin, L. R. (1942) *The Public Library System of Great Britain: a report on its present condition with proposals for post-war reorganization*, London, Library Association (the McColvin Report).

Roberts, S. C. (1959) Great Britain, Ministry of Education, *The Structure Of The Public Library Service In England And Wales: report of the committee appointed by the Minister of Education in September 1957*, London, HMSO (the Roberts Report).

Toft, Z. (2004) What Librarians Can Do For Us: an academic's perspective, *Library and Information Update*, **3** (1), January, 42–3.

Privatisation Raises Concerns (2005) Privatisation Raises Concerns, *Library and Information Update*, **4** (1–2), January/February, 3.

2 Recruitment, supervision, education and training

This chapter is about the people who organize and run library services and about their selection, training and responsibilities. It will address issues about structures and relationships, rights and responsibilities, and will seek to inform about formal and informal structures.

The recruitment process

The quality of any library service can be said to rest upon two foundations: the quality and commitment of the staff and the support and resources provided by the governing body responsible for the service. Too often the former covers for deficiencies in the latter! It follows from this that the selection, appointment, training, development and leadership of the people within the service are critical matters.

For many years the first stage in recruitment was to advertise the post. Given all the pressures on modern libraries and information units, the first step these days is to look hard and long to see if indeed there is a post to fill and, if so, whether a different job description is now necessary. This approach allows the librarian to:

- decide if there is a post to be filled
- re-evaluate the existing post to discover if a different job specification is necessary
- review the qualifications required
- review the type of person required.

Yes, there is a danger that this will slow down the appointment process, but since recruitment is a costly matter, getting it right saves time and money in the longer term. So, what are the steps that might be taken to ensure a good appointment?

Consultation

There should be consultation not only with senior managers and the Human Resources Department, but also with those supervising the post and those with whom the new person will work. Managers will usually seek the views of the present postholder about what the job currently entails. They will decide who needs to be at the interview.

Specification

Usually the specification covers both the job and the person. Fitting individuals into a team may require special qualities. Educational and training qualifications will be important in a person specification, as will experience. Choosing the right person is greatly aided by a good job specification and person specification.

Recruitment policy

Many employers try to promote first from internal candidates before advertising externally. Draft job/personal descriptions and advertisements will need to be checked by the Human Resources Department for compliance with legal and employer policies. Awareness of, and compliance with, equal opportunities legislation is particularly important.

The legal bases of equal opportunities in the UK include the Equal Pay Act (1970), the Sex Discrimination Act (1975), the Race Relations Act (1976; amendments 2000), the European Directive on Racial Discrimination (2000) and the Disability Discrimination Act (1995). Additionally, it is hoped that there will be some age discrimination legislation in 2006.

Where to advertise

Where the advertisement is placed will vary according to the type of post being filled. It may be in the local papers, the national and professional press or announced through job centres.

The job description

Creating a job description is important since it helps to ensure that the work is really appropriate to the tasks required and the person appointed. It allows supervisors and managers to monitor progress and feeds into any staff development or appraisal scheme. It can become helpful in settling disputes about workloads and duties but should never be so tightly drawn as to be inflexible. The job description should:

- aid recruitment
- help future training
- define the boundaries of the post
- state line management routes and reporting levels
- help ensure that major tasks are covered
- list duties/tasks.

When preparing job descriptions it is very important to consider carefully the factors relating to the type of job being offered. When deciding whether a job is professional or not, the manager should check the various items that make up the profile of the task against what a professional librarian should theoretically be doing. Clearly at the borderlines or in a small library it will be difficult to keep things so clear cut, since some posts will have to combine both professional and paraprofessional work. However, the skill of the personnel officer can keep these ambiguous posts to the absolute minimum. It may well be that by looking at the duties involved in several posts together, they can be so organized as to make it easier to delineate professional from paraprofessional duties across the range of posts in the service.

Often the title of the post can help clear the mind. Reference librarian, readers' services librarian, chief cataloguer or subject specialist all give the clear starting point of a professional post. Problems arise in parapro-fessional posts where some of the tasks may sound, or in fact be, similar. The cut-off point between a professional cataloguer and an assistant who checks databases for records, or updates basic records, is more complex and the assistant could, depending on other duties, fall either side of the divide. In the UK the middle ground comprises staff who have taken courses like the City and Guilds Library and Information Services Progression Award Level 3, or the Information and Library Services NVQ 3. These are the staff who will be in CILIP's Affiliated Members group; they are the link staff in the library structure. In some countries this type of post is called 'library technician'. Some of the qualifications mentioned are obtainable in the UK by distance learning methods (see below in the Training section).

Application forms

Most libraries use a standard application form. This is helpful since it captures common information and makes comparisons more cost effective. It should also ensure that all candidates are asked to provide identical information and should, therefore, eliminate the possibility of discrimination. It is increasingly the case that Human Resources Departments ensure that information about ethnic origins, and often gender information, is not available to the shortlisting panel.

Shortlisting

This is the next stage and is often the most difficult. Many seemingly good applicants must be set aside since the number that can be interviewed must be limited. It is essential that the criteria for selecting for interview are clear and applied fairly. Often the shortlist comprises only six or seven candidates. It is important that those creating the shortlist recognize that one of these people will soon be a member of staff and so the organization must start relationships off in the correct manner.

Responding to applications

Recruitment is part of the public image of a library service. This image is created partly by how we treat applicants. Prompt acknowledgement of job applications, sympathetic rejection letters to unsuccessful candidates, and clear invitations to interview are all important. Candidates require notice of the time and location of interviews (they may need to arrange absence from existing employers).

The interview

The object of the interview is to enable the two parties to assess each other, so that when a post is offered the employer has selected a candidate who actually wants to do the job. To achieve this end, the method of interview has to be structured to overcome the totally artificial atmosphere that can so easily be created. This is not to say that the formal interview across a table has no place in selection procedures, since the stress it normally occasions can often occur in real work situations.

The following methods can be employed to give candidates a more balanced interview and also to involve more of the library staff in the interview.

Practical arrangements

Reception staff need to be informed of the names of interviewees and times of interviews (and of any delays), waiting areas with reading matter need to be provided and the location of cloakrooms indicated. Refreshment should be offered if any delay occurs.

The interview room should be arranged to provide a relaxed atmosphere to encourage openness. Never ask candidates to drink and talk at the same time – offering a drink during the actual interview may sound kind but is not!

Workplace tour

This is intended to enable candidates to look at the physical surroundings in which they would be working, and to give them a chance to talk informally with members of staff performing functions similar to those involved in the job for which they are applying. It is helpful to involve senior library assistants, who can talk with candidates informally, either in a group or individually, and who will often form useful impressions of their suitability. These views should be passed to the interviewing panel to form part of the overall assessment of each applicant's suitability for the post.

Formal interviews

The formal interview, in which the candidate faces a panel, often comprising the librarian, the personnel officer and a few other individuals, is traditional. All too often the size of the interviewing panel is out of all proportion to the salary being offered for the job advertised and, while it may be appropriate to have half a dozen people interviewing for a senior professional post, two or three are quite adequate for more junior posts.

When conducting these interviews the chairperson should always allow a settling-in period in which the candidate answers relatively simple, general questions before the session focuses on more essential matters.

In formulating the more relevant questions to ask the candidate the interviewers have three basic tools to assist them: the interviewee's application form, the job description and the personal description. When examining how closely the applicant's history and qualifications match up to the personal description, areas that need to be explored normally become evident.

Towards the end of the time available for the interview, there should be an opportunity for the candidate to ask questions of the panel. Often these questions will be related to such matters as salary, conditions of service and starting dates, but there will occasionally be more interesting questions, and these may well give an insight into the character of the applicant.

The expert interviewer will make notes on his or her feelings about each applicant relating to individual areas of questioning, so that by the end of the interviewing session there are sufficient notes to allow a fair assessment of the candidates.

Increasingly, candidates are asked to give appropriate presentations as part of the interview process. This may be just to the interviewing panel, but could also be to a group of potential colleagues. Careful preparation is required, and confidence can be boosted by trial runs to friends and family. It is very important to be entirely familiar with any aids used, particularly electronic ones.

It is worth noting that presentations are not just tools for assessing candidates. Any paraprofessional who is serious about career progression must expect to be able to give presentations to fellow members of staff when called upon to do so, for example when reporting back on conferences or training events attended.

Group interviews

This technique is normally used only when filling higher professional posts, but is occasionally used for posts at other levels. Here the candidates are brought together and given the opportunity to join a general discussion with members of the interviewing panel. This can be an extremely helpful technique when used in the appropriate circumstances. Peer group assessment is an increasingly used tool in appointing new staff. It is after all very important that the views of colleagues with whom the candidate will work if appointed are taken into consideration.

The candidate's preparations

As a candidate, always think about the job, the employer and what the employer might be looking for when making the appointment. It is easy to get quite detailed information about employers from such documents as annual reports, council offices and registers. This helps you to build up a picture and get ready for the questions at interview.

Always plan for the day of the interview. Check the route and transport arrangements; try to find out the format of the interview; ensure that you dress appropriately; prepare for some of the basic questions by asking yourself:

- Why am I the best candidate?
- Why am I seeking to leave my present post?
- What can I contribute to this service?
- What is my management/supervisory style?
- What do I know about this service?
- What are my social attributes and abilities?

Performing well

At the interview there are steps that you can take to help success:

- Arrive in good time and relax.
- Use positive body language: smile, do not slouch, look alert and make eye contact.
- Shake hands.
- Do not fidget: sit calmly.
- Answer questions clearly and succinctly: do not ramble.
- Give positive examples of your past achievements: say 'I did . . .' or 'We did . . .'
- Do not interrupt or overreact to questions.
- Do not criticize your existing employers.
- Do not evade issues.
- Be ready with good questions: What training is provided? Are there promotion opportunities? And so on.

Induction

An essential requirement for all new postholders, whether paraprofessional or professional, is appropriate induction into the service, where new staff meet colleagues and see how each department relates to the others. The induction procedure must occur immediately after the postholder joins the organization, otherwise bad habits may form which will be difficult to eradicate.

The induction course will cover:

• all the necessary employment details and conditions of service
• the leave entitlement
• an explanation of the contract of employment, insurance stoppages (monies automatically taken from salaries in the UK to pay PAYE and national insurance dues) and other such matters
• an indication of what to do in case of sickness and who to inform when unable to attend for duty.

Equally importantly, it will provide a background to the social structure of the library: the staff guild, any clubs or unions that operate within the organization, discount schemes, car parking facilities, arrangements for meals and so on.

This early opportunity should also be taken to impress upon the new entrant the right attitudes to work and to the public. Much of this information is best reinforced by the production of a staff handbook that can be given to every new entrant. The handbook should also contain a list of the staff and an explanation of the departmental structures, so that relationships can be learned easily and the right people contacted from the outset.

The management structure

One of the issues often forgotten in the induction process is an explanation of the management structure of the whole service and the part within it that applies to the new member of staff.

Formal structures are important, even though the organization may pride itself upon being open and friendly. Staff need to know who is responsible for each major activity and how they report to one another. Without this formality it is possible for a new member of staff to begin to resent being led by another since their personal relationship, in terms of supervision or management, may never have been made clear. In this situation both parties suffer. In fact, most of us have organizational charts, many with the names as well as job titles clearly stated upon them. This tree of the organization is easy to produce and really helps to show newcomers the shape of an organization. It encourages communication through the best channels, and aids proper management of a service.

Informal structures always exist and good supervisors soon get to know about them – frequently use them in a constructive fashion. Often among a team of assistants one stands out and becomes an unofficial leader, and this person can represent the group to the officially appointed leader. This is more common the larger the span of management given to an individual – the more staff s/he manages, the less time each gets, so the more useful it can be to tap into informal structures.

Perhaps the greatest informal structure is the rumour mill that exists in every organization. It is amazing how these work, but they do, and often the information is both correct and early! Good management links, team briefings and so on can all help to put supervisors and managers back in control of the communication process.

The value of induction

Induction can be said to ensure that new employees:

- are integrated with other staff
- understand the employer's culture and approaches
- are aware of the skills and knowledge required to perform their tasks
- are productive and motivated
- recognize that they are valued individuals
- understand the structure of the organization.

The probationary period

In most organizations in the UK new entrants are employed for a probationary period. The length of probation may well vary, but its purpose is to enable the employer and the employee to assess one another. Obviously if the employee is dissatisfied with the job he or she will look for another post. If there is dissatisfaction with the way the employee is responding to training the employer may well wish to consider invoking the probation clause in the letter of appointment. If this is to be done, it is important that adequate warnings be given to the employee throughout the period of probation. These should include written warnings indicating very clearly the areas where dissatisfaction is being occasioned. It is equally important that additional training is given to give the employee further opportunity to improve performance. Copies of all correspondence must be included in the individual's personal file.

Training, education and personal and professional development for paraprofessional library staff

After the initial training provided by the induction process (see above), it is sensible for the newly appointed paraprofessional to explore as many aspects of formal and informal development as possible. Indeed, staff at all levels should be given on-going training and development opportunities.

Most organizations have come to realize the value of staff development during recent years – indeed it is government policy that they do so. The UK's Chartermark initiatives and developments such as Investors in People, as well as current staff appraisal policies, have clear staff training and development implications. We have seen the attitudes of organizations to training and development change from what in many cases was mere lip service to the concept to a real commitment.

It is important to note that throughout this section we are using the term 'training' to imply skills-based and vocational development, whereas 'education' implies a wider approach and pertains to the whole person rather than just to the person as employee.

We will deal first with appropriate initial in-service training. For example, a new employee about to take up duties in a public library using a computerized issue system will clearly need some training in advance.

'On-the-job' training also usually takes place during the initial period. This is usually informal and can be undertaken by experienced colleagues at the same level, or by the line manager.

Shadowing colleagues, secondment or job exchanges may follow later. Job exchanges are most likely to be offered to professionally qualified staff – see the excellent article by Jonathan Tindale on exchanging jobs from a City context to a rural library in New Zealand (Tindale, 2004).

Libex, the International Library and Information Exchange, provides useful information for those contemplating such a move, and can be contacted by e-mail (angela.frampton@cilip.org.uk).

The present writer has arranged brief job exchanges at paraprofessional level as part of delivering paraprofessional courses, and they proved to offer very useful training opportunities.

In-service training

This may take many forms. For example, in large county library systems new library assistants may spend a period in each of the departments to familiarize themselves with the totality of the service.

Local authority library staff in the UK normally have the opportunity to attend appropriate LEA courses (for example, customer care or telephone enquiry techniques) which are relevant to their jobs but not specific to library and information work. The library/information unit itself may have a rolling programme of courses on more specific library skills, such as organizing displays, story reading to children or running reader groups, which all staff will have an opportunity to attend at some point.

Outside bodies such as commercial binderies or the British Library often put on suitable day courses, and CILIP itself is an excellent provider of appropriate courses at both local and national level.

The issue of *Library and Information Gazette* current at the time of writing (February 2005) gives details of courses such as a workshop on enquiry skills 'Giving a good answer', which would clearly be useful to staff across a range of levels/posts, and, with an emphasis more on professionally qualified staff, a practical workshop on 'The innovative use of physical space for knowledge' (see www.cilip.org.uk/training).

We must not forget the great value of attending appropriate conferences, which provide a wonderful opportunity for networking and for exchanging views and information. Most of the special groups of CILIP hold extremely useful annual or biennial conferences.

Paraprofessional library staff in the UK are currently in a greatly improving situation with regard to access to the type of training discussed in this section. For example ICT training has been increasingly available to library staff over the last few years, funded by the New Opportunities Fund. This initiative is now ending, but the majority of public library paraprofessional staff, and some school library staff, have successfully completed courses such as the European Computer Driving Licence.

When considering wider educational and personal development, there are opportunities such as those provided by the Open University and by adult education evening classes. It is the present writer's belief that library staff who seek personal development in this way bring something extra and very valuable to their work even though the courses they have pursued may not have specific relevance to library and information work.

Formal professional and paraprofessional education and training

We now turn to formal professional and paraprofessional education and training in the UK – a field where, since the last edition of this book, great and far-reaching changes have taken place.

Traditionally, CILIP (formerly The Library Association) concentrated on professional library and information education, validating the first degree courses in library and information studies in UK universities, and the postgraduate MScs and diplomas, as well as laying down procedures for admittance to the Charter following completion of one of the CILIP qualifications. Paraprofessional education was largely outside CILIP's remit, though the then Library Association did oversee the introduction of the Information and Library Services NVQs in 1995. There has been a very clear divide between professional and paraprofessional, in terms of training, status, salary and work undertaken.

When the present writer first began teaching paraprofessional library and information courses in the UK some 15 years ago, it was striking that not all, but a majority of students operating at paraprofessional level were desirous of, and indeed completely capable of, proceeding to professional status and Chartership had the opportunities for doing this without a full-time three-year degree course not been minimal. Most of the students were (and still are) women, often with heavy domestic and financial responsibilities, who were never going to be able to cross the barrier between paraprofessional and professional because of these factors, and who were thus depriving the sector of competent and experienced staff more than capable of operating at professional level.

All this is changing and CILIP is embracing all levels of library and information staff in its new Framework of Qualifications (Spring 2005), which means that potentially all library and information workers who provide evidence of professional potential and who wish to proceed to Chartership will have the opportunity to do so. The Framework combines the maintenance of high professional standards of education and training with a widening of opportunities, and is in line with current government thinking on the continuous upskilling of the workforce (*Library and Information Update*, 2004). Further details of the CILIP Framework are available at www.cilip.org.uk/qualifications-chartership.

The Framework covers all levels, but we will concentrate on its relevance to the paraprofessional. For the first time, paraprofessionals who are members of the Affiliated Members Group of CILIP have a means of acquiring formal certification as ACLIPs (Associates of the Chartered Institute of Library and Information Professionals). Experiential learning gained in a work context, qualifications such as the Information and Library Services NVQ Level 3 (ILS-NVQ3) or the City & Guilds Library and Information Services Progression Award Level 3 (City and Guilds 7371) all count, and there is a portfolio building approach.

The ILS-NVQs follow a portfolio-based approach of evidence built up in the workplace and assessed by qualified assessors. City and Guilds 7371 is at the same level as the ILS-NVQ3, but is assessed both practically (five practical assignments consisting of portfolios of evidence and practical tasks) and theoretically (four written theory papers), thus providing a broader approach.

We should also mention Modern Apprenticeships, which require candidates to achieve the ILS-NVQ3 and (to provide the underpinning knowledge) City and Guilds 7371, while employed under an apprenticeship scheme.

There are clear routes to Chartership for those staff who wish to follow them, and there is also official recognition of the contribution made to the sector by paraprofessional staff. For fuller details of the new Framework, the CILIP *Certification Scheme Handbook* may be consulted.

To conclude this section on training and education, we very much welcome the opening of new opportunities for all library staff, bridging the great divide between professional and paraprofessional education and training which stems from the 1960s, and the maintenance of clear and rigorous standards of education and training within the sector.

Summary of staff recruitment, retention and development

1 Staff selection should represent the start of a continuous process of development. At the interview, identification of an individual's needs commences, as does identification of what should be done to maximize that person's ability to do the tasks associated with the appointment.

2 Induction is the process by which new postholders are integrated into the service, so that they become active, co-operative and productive members of staff as soon as possible. Induction may be a single event in the early days of employment or, as many organizations prefer, a short foundation at the start with call-up events over the first few months.

This latter method has the advantage of setting the scene initially while allowing for questions to form following practice.

3 Training is a means of equipping staff to perform their tasks competently and efficiently, and to adopt suitable attitudes that are central to, unique to or desired by the service. Much training will be in-house, drawn from a set list of topics and repeated on a regular basis. Examples are training in the operation of issue systems, customer care and telephone technique.

4 Staff development is generally regarded as moving staff on through a range of educational activities and so improving their performance. Attendance at certificated courses and conferences, reskilling for changing work opportunities and so on all fall within this category.

5 Educational development challenges the individual in fundamental ways. It also covers the assessment of an organization's requirement for all the above issues and can offer solutions to staff needs through consultancy. Educational development is generally thought to cover a number of functions relating to the enhancement of the major approaches and needs of a service. It is often regarded as including the co-ordination and overseeing of policies, procedures and quality assurance as well as general advice and support for all aspects of development, delivery, assessment and evaluation.

6 Staff manuals and handbooks are important tools for helping new staff fit into an organization. The handbook usually provides information about the employer and employment regulations, opportunities for union membership, social activities and other such matters. The staff manual is a more work-based document and should contain detailed advice on how to operate key equipment, appropriate approaches to inquiries, staff to seek help from in case of conflict, procedures in general use and special conditions that might apply in single locations – in short, a sort of guide to practice that the new recruit can turn to when in doubt.

Supervisory duties

Supervision is the art of leadership. It is difficult to define clearly but it provides the bond between management and the workers. As far as possible a good supervisor should involve the team in determining objectives, choosing working methods, organizing work schedules, problem solving and decision making. This is not an abrogation of responsibility but a way of getting the best from a group of staff. A wise supervisor should remember that within the team there may be people with a closer understanding of a particular issue than his or her own. Success as a supervisor requires an understanding of what makes people 'tick', particularly as far as work is concerned.

Supervisors should:

- communicate well
- show commitment to the service
- help empower their staff
- get the best out of staff
- listen to staff
- be approachable
- know the staff and their concerns.

The most essential part of the supervisor's task is to lead the library assistants and show them how their job fits into the wider service. The supervisor will perform a range of tasks depending upon the individual library but some generic tasks are:

- developing timetables
- managing workloads
- training
- reviewing the operation of service points
- advising management
- balancing duties daily
- conveying and explaining decisions
- passing information upwards
- building the team.

Once upon a time work was regarded as a necessary evil but this attitude has changed as more people regard work as both an enjoyable and a fulfilling part of their lives. Those supervising need to remember that their colleagues work for a number of reasons:

- to gain material comfort
- for recognition and prestige
- for challenge and interest.

If these needs can be fulfilled then it follows that all will benefit from greater enjoyment and job satisfaction. Productivity will increase and so will positive attitudes towards users.

Some of the steps a supervisor can take to lift colleagues from minimal performance to more effective standards include helping them to:

- realize that work is a satisfying part of life and not just the bit that earns money
- develop clear targets through which their performance can be measured
- consider incentives
- keep informed of changes so that they feel more secure
- see your respect for them as individuals
- feel that you monitor working conditions for safety and comfort
- recognize that you value them as team members.

Communication

One word above all others is the key to being a good supervisor. That word is communication. Communication comes naturally to some: the rest of us need to think about it and develop the skills. The greatest difficulty with communication is making it happen. Most supervisors will intend to let people know all they need to know, but this may remain no more than an intention until a communication method is set up and implemented. In the following parts of this chapter we talk about structures to achieve this, and they should be taken to heart by any supervisor.

At a more basic level we need to consider the three main methods of communication available within the workplace. These are oral, written and visual:

1 Oral: formal and informal meetings and interviews, telephone conversations and casual conversations (management by walkabout!). Oral communication is very immediate and allows questions to be asked to clarify understanding. However, there is a lack of permanence, no record exists and outcomes will soon be forgotten. For important information it is always helpful to follow up with a written note.

2 Written: letters, notes, memos, reports, notice boards, manuals, e-mail and so on. The problem with written communication is that the writer is not there when it is read and questions cannot be answered before misunderstanding takes place. You cannot be sure that the paper has arrived or, indeed, that if it has arrived it has been read. Written

communications in isolation bring problems and should be supported by face-to-face sessions.

3 Visual: non-verbal signs are interesting and can tell the supervisor a lot about how a message is being received. Glazed eyes, agitated movement and excitement all indicate that questions ought to be posed so that full understanding, on both sides, can be achieved.

Meetings

Perhaps the most-used form of oral communication, linked to written communication, that we use is the meeting. Supervisors and managers spend more time in meetings than is, perhaps, good for them or the service! If we are to spend so much time in this way it is important that we plan and prepare for meetings so that they achieve results that justify their costs.

Often supervisors will chair meetings. The chair has particular responsibilities to be clear about the objectives of the meeting and who should attend. S/he must also ensure that a clear timetable is established so that all the items can be covered while allowing members present an opportunity to contribute. The basic stages of planning a good meeting can be summarized as:

- Prepare: be clear about the objectives and how to achieve them.
- Plan: create a clear agenda with enough detail to ensure that people arrive understanding what the item really means.
- Appoint someone to take minutes.
- Book: ensure that a room is available for the duration of the meeting and that any refreshments are ordered and their delivery time agreed.
- Start on time: always start promptly even if not all have arrived. Do not punish the punctual for those who turn up late!
- Involve everyone: encourage all to contribute. In most meetings you will have shy people: try to bring them into the discussions.
- Control the meeting: make all contributions come 'through the chair'. This stops cross talking and second meetings starting.
- Summarize decisions: before leaving an agenda item outline where you think the meeting is on the matter. Issue action details to individuals and allocate timescales for action.
- Follow up: refer to the minutes and ensure that they contain all the agreed action points. Check later that action is being taken or reports prepared for a future meeting.

- Evaluate: did the meeting work? Did you achieve the objectives? Did anyone get left out? Were the right people present?

Customer care

Part of a supervisor's duties will be to understand and monitor any customer care arrangements that the service has devised. Successful customer care is really about making the customer or user want to come back again. One organization describes its programme as not just meeting customer expectations but 'delighting' them by ensuring that all staff treat them with friendliness and positive approaches.

Interestingly enough the large commercial companies, who started the customer care movement, claim that a good implementation not only makes users want to return but also increases staff motivation, since the working environment seems to improve.

Supervisors are at the heart of customer care. They are close to the action and can see and hear what is going on. How they act will determine how all staff act and, therefore, the success of the scheme. A good scheme requires top management support and formal codes of conduct. Training will be essential, as will supervision of the implementation of the plan.

Libraries and information units are very like commercial companies when it comes to customer care, in that both have external customers and internal customers. Remember that in all libraries some of the users also work for the organization, in other departments. So in designing customer care we need to investigate what users really need: in some respects we cover this in Chapter 5. However, it is perhaps helpful to summarize it here in different words. The range of approaches to establish customer needs includes:

- feedback directly from customers
- direct discussions with customers
- attitude surveys
- focus groups
- analysis of complaints and comments
- looking at physical premises.

From this it is possible to develop performance standards and formalize them after discussion with staff and customers. Once agreed they need to be communicated to both staff and customers and then evaluated regularly. Some of the standards that might be developed are:

- times queues take to clear
- time taken to answer the phone
- time between reservations and supply
- quality and speed of information delivered
- book to shelf return times.

Motivation

Supervisors need at least a little understanding of motivation and behaviour. Perhaps we could summarize this as a recognition that every employee has needs. These will vary, not only from person to person, but also from time to time with each person.

According to A. H. Maslow's (1970) theory of human motivation, there are five levels of need:

1 Physical needs: these are often associated with bodily comfort. It is therefore important for the supervisor to take into account such matters as comfortable room temperatures, the freshness of the air and the adequacy of ventilation, levels of lighting, decoration and canteen facilities.
2 Security needs: security is a basic need for most people since it applies both to employment and to home life. From the supervisor's point of view it is worth bearing in mind that to exercise disciplinary control through threats may well be self-defeating since these threats will attack this basic need for security.
3 Social needs: these include such things as acceptance by fellow workers and integration into the informal structures of the organization.
4 Esteem needs: these cover not only how individuals see their own role but also the perception of how others see them. This need can be recognized by offering criticism only in private but giving praise in public.
5 Self-actualization: or, the need to realize one's potential. Training, education and promotion all play their parts in this need.

A basic understanding of what motivates each individual helps a supervisor plan the right approach. Generally it is sound to assume competence, to involve people in decision making and to take opinions into account – this helps to create an atmosphere of trust, harmony and co-operation. Where problems do arise it is sensible to check out the training programme before blaming, say, the assistant for poor performance of duties. However, if after full investigation it is found that the assistant has been trained properly and is capable of performing the duties accurately, but is just not performing them satisfactorily, it is essential that the supervisor takes the assistant aside and attempts to discover the reasons for the problems, then tries to overcome them. It could sometimes be of help to use the services of welfare or personnel officers since, often, people will talk to outsiders rather more easily than they can talk to their immediate superiors. Supervisors do have an important responsibility to the organization and if, in spite of all this care and attention, there are still staff who are causing problems – because they were selected for the wrong job, because they feel some sense of grievance and are therefore being obstructive or because they are just not able to handle certain tasks – the supervisor has a clear responsibility to give adequate warnings as to future conduct, to ensure further training is given, to follow this up with written warnings and, if necessary, make contact with union representatives.

Keeping records

From all of the foregoing the need to keep clear, confidential records will be apparent. Accuracy of information is vital and particular care must be taken to record joining dates, changes of post, salary levels and so forth, promptly and correctly. Only appropriate staff will be allowed access to these files, since they contain very sensitive information. Staff who do have access must be selected for their discretion and must never use their knowledge except in the performance of their duties. Increasingly libraries are moving to computerized personnel systems and the effects of any data protection laws that are in force in your country may be such that accuracy and confidentiality are even more important, since employees can take legal action if records used for promotion, reference and such like are not fully up to date. Under the UK Data Protection Act employees have the right to see data held on them and to ask for it to be corrected if necessary. Failure to do this could lead to an unlimited fine if the matter is taken to court.

Some libraries prefer to keep to paper records, which can be in two forms. The first is a simple card that contains the 'core' details of each employee. This is supported by an individual file that contains copies of all documents regarding the individual from the time he or she first applied for the post. The file will start with the job description and personal description and will also contain copies of the advertisement, the completed application form, the references taken up, comments recorded during interview and the letter of appointment. Once the new member is in post, any letters relating to changes in conditions of employment, letters of commendation or warnings as to future conduct will be placed in the file. The file will obviously normally be closed when the employee leaves the organization, though it will usually be kept in store for several years, after which time it may well be microcopied and stored as an archive on a CD-ROM; the original may then be destroyed. The reason for keeping the file in its original state for a few years after the member of staff has left is that quite often that person will give their former employer's name as a referee. Copies of any references given should be added to the file.

The second type of record is more organizationally based and shows staff by department or section. This helps managers in ensuring that appraisal and staff development interviews are carried out by an appropriate manager.

Obviously automation extends the usefulness of staff records, since by careful encoding of information personnel officers can achieve useful statistical comparisons – for example, the number of staff who have a certain qualification, training dates and results, promotion points and so on.

Conclusion

We hope that the above overview of recruitment, supervision, education, training and development will be useful to staff in employment and to those seeking changes of direction within the library and information sector.

References

Library and Information Update (2004) *Launched: certification and ethics framework*, **3** (9), September, 17–18.

Maslow, A. H. (1970) *Motivation and Personality*, 2nd edn, New York, Harper and Row.

Tindale, J. (2004) Exchanging Jobs, *Library and Information Update*, **3** (5), May, 22–5.

3 Library co-operation in the UK

General introduction

By the 1920s and 1930s it was becoming clear that the individual libraries of the now firmly established public library service could no longer on their own meet the demands of an increasingly educated clientèle in a context of rapidly developing knowledge and the resulting huge increase in the number of books published.

The need for the establishment of co-operative networks involving all types of library service, academic and special as well as public, was established by the *Kenyon Report* of 1927. Frederick Kenyon chaired the Public Library Committee, whose brief had been to inquire into the adequacy of public library provision and the means of extending it. A series of recommendations concerning co-operation featured in the report, leading to the establishment of the National Central Library in 1931, and the setting up of the Regional Library Bureaux (RLB) in the 1930s.

Various national initiatives, such as the setting up of the National Lending Library for Science and Technology (1962) and the National Reference Library of Science and Invention (both of which, together with the National Central Library, became part of the British Library in 1973), followed over the next decades. Also at a national level, Aslib (the Association of Special Libraries and Information Bureaux), founded in 1924, was promoting special library co-operation throughout this period.

However, it was arguably at a local level that the most important developments in library co-operation took place, with a number of significant schemes being introduced during the 1940s, 1950s and 1960s. Many of these local schemes are still with us today and still promoting co-operation in a range of areas at local level.

At a time when the information needs of industry, academic research and the general public are increasing rapidly, while at the same time libraries of most types are experiencing severe financial restrictions, it is essential that local initiatives such as these continue to flourish alongside the national formal interlending structures of the Regional Library Bureaux and the British Library Document Supply Centre (BLDSC).

The Regional Library Bureaux

For the purposes of library interlending and formal co-operation, the British Isles are organized into nine regions. Scotland, Ireland and Wales each form a region, and England is divided into six regions: Northern, Yorkshire and Humberside, East Midlands, South Western, West Midlands, and North Western. LASER, the London and South-East Region, has now ceased to operate in its traditional role and has become a grant-making trust with a general remit. Recent initiatives deal with the setting up of regional development agencies but it is to be hoped that these would strengthen RLBs rather than replace them.

The vital partner in library interlending is the British Library Document Supply Centre (BLDSC). The regions themselves are linked by the Circle of Officers of National and Regional Library Systems (CONARLS), through which the managers of regional library systems, together with other appropriate personnel, meet regularly.

Most of the Regional Library Bureaux were established in the 1930s, and many of them have recently celebrated their diamond jubilees. They have established both the principle and the practice of efficient and effective interlending, enabling users from the smallest and most obscure service points to access, via themselves or the BLDSC, the vast lending stock of the entire country. Often on very limited budgets and with very few staff, the RLB have provided a model of the valuable co-operation that is possible within a sector. However, there is some evidence that formal national library interlending is entering a period of change and uncertainty, which can in part be attributed to the application of business ethics to a service industry. The Bureaux are currently operating in a context of changing and reducing membership, compulsory business plans, changing charge structures at both local and national (BLDSC) levels, potential elements of privatization and tendering out. There is, however, a real determination that the individual reader, whose needs have been so admirably met for so many years, should not suffer from the current changes and uncertainty. The existence of formal interlibrary lending schemes means that users of the smallest and remotest library and information units have equal access to the lending resources of the country with users of large city libraries.

For the purposes of this chapter we shall be using the South Western Regional Library System (SWRLS) as our case study. SWRLS was founded in 1937 to promote library co-operation and interlending in the region. Membership consists of county libraries, unitary authority libraries, university libraries, college libraries and special libraries. There has been a decline in membership, particularly that of special libraries, in recent years.

The library co-operation promoted by SWRLS is financed by a population-based subscription from the public libraries, and an annual subscription plus a charge per item borrowed from non-county libraries, with account taken of the difference between items borrowed and items lent. The cost of a regionally supplied interlibrary loan is between £4 and £5, with local variations. SWRLS operates from Bristol Central Library, but the staff salaries and employers' costs are repaid to Bristol by SWRLS.

SWRLS, in common with the other regional systems, offers a range of co-operative services. Foremost of these are the interlending services, greatly facilitated by the Unity database. Member libraries inform the bureau of their accessions and last-copy deletions by International Standard Book Number (ISBN) on a regular basis. SWRLS encourages those member libraries with complete automated catalogues to contribute to Unity.

Unity was originally developed as a PC-based system in partnership with LNW (Libraries North West). Six other regions joined the project, which is partnered by Talis Information Ltd. A very significant development occurred when Unityweb went online in 2001, with more than 10 million records and more than 35 million locations, indicated by number codes. This has not only speeded up the request process – libraries can e-mail interlibrary loans to each other, and use ARTEmail to BLDSC (ART (Automated Request Transmission) is a means of sending ILL requests to the British Library via e-mail (ARTEmail), web (ARTWeb) or telecommunications (ARTTel)) – but its user-friendliness also means that it can be used by the general public (www.swrls.org.uk/unity.htm).

Unity covers Wales, Scotland and most of England, and also provides some additional databases including the complete British National Bibliography file.

SWRLS uses HaysDX, the South West Transport Scheme, to transport books around the region, and is promoting WISDOM, an initiative which joins up library catalogues to facilitate finding and locating for the general public.

Borrowing from other libraries

At a practical level, typical procedures involved in borrowing from or lending to libraries within a regional co-operative system are as follows:

1 A request for an item is received from a library user; a check in the catalogue and in the 'on-order' file reveals that it is not in current library stock or on order for stock.
2 The bibliographical details of the requested item are checked for completeness and accuracy.
3 The Unity database is accessed and, typically, three regional locations are noted.
4 A pro forma containing the full details plus a rota of holding libraries may be sent to the first location; increasingly, however, telephone or e-mail may be used, and it may be that printed pro formas will eventually be phased out.
5 The first location will supply if immediately available; other options are to reserve the item if it is on loan but due back shortly, or to contact the next library on the rota list. All libraries may decline to lend valuable or in-demand material.
6 A subsequent location will normally supply the item, although a percentage of requests are difficult to fulfil, in which case BLDSC may be approached. Many BL locations are given in Unity.

When dealing with interlibrary loans it is important that there are precise and accurate recording procedures in operation. In libraries such as university libraries, dealing with thousands of interlibrary loans per year, this information may be put on computer.

It is very important for the efficiency of the service that all interlibrary loans are regularly chased, that the date and result of the chase (for example 'third on waiting list') is noted, and that requesters are always kept completely up to date with the progress of their request. Statistics must always be kept of all interlibrary lending and borrowing, and a record of the return of borrowed items should be retained against the possibility of loss in transit.

Lending to other libraries

There are also procedures involved in supplying an interlibrary loan to another library within the region:

1 Requests are received by fax, phone, e-mail or post
2 A ticket is made for the requesting library (or a computer card in the case of libraries with computerized systems) and the item issued in the normal way, although it is usual to allow a longer loan period. The item is subject to normal overdue, renewal and reservation procedures.
3 Statistics are kept to generate payment (as explained earlier in this chapter).
4 The item is sent to the requesting library, through the nationwide van system.

Purchase and storage schemes

Like most regional systems, SWRLS operates co-operative purchase and storage schemes, whereby member libraries guarantee to purchase and retain all stock in specified subject areas. Where fiction is concerned, SWRLS is part of the Provincial Joint Fiction Reserve – member libraries currently buy and retain fiction by authors whose surnames begin T–Z. Since 1980, junior fiction has also been covered in this way. Non-fiction is covered similarly using Dewey classification numbers (for example, within the South-Western regional area, Gloucestershire buys every British book on glass technology 666.2). SWRLS also participates in the Subject Specialization scheme, Encore, which is an online database for music locations, the Plymouth Music Scheme, and Newsplan, a nationwide project aimed at ensuring the availability of local newspapers on microfilm (www.swrls.org.uk/).

The British Library Document Supply Centre

We discussed in Chapter 1 the British Library as a national library. In this chapter we will concentrate on the British Library Document Supply Centre, situated in Boston Spa in West Yorkshire.

The BLDSC is the hub of national and international interlending. It is the largest supplier of documents in the world, supplying both individuals and libraries from its vast collection of material. It currently dispatches around four million documents per year, satisfying over 90% of demand, either from its own vast collection or through other back-up libraries.

The main criterion for acquisition of an item by the BLDSC is whether the item is likely to be requested by clients in business and industry, higher education and research, though a more general demand is also met. A few categories, such as in-print fiction, are generally excluded from the service. Documents or loans are usually obtained by individuals via their libraries. A major feature is the supply of photocopied periodical articles – a vast international research collection is held – and a new electronic delivery service means that requesters can receive the documents they need within a few hours

Requesting from the BLDSC

There is now a variety of ways in which libraries may request material from the BLDSC on behalf of their users. A decision to use the BLDSC is normally taken when the item concerned is unavailable locally or through the appropriate Regional Library Bureaux. Many libraries have a policy of always using the BLDSC to supply photocopies of periodical articles because of their speed and wide coverage. Requests are normally made by ART (Automated Request Transmission), often via ARTTel and ARTEmail. Methods of payment have recently changed: clients have a deposit account with BLDSC paid in advance and a billing account paid in arrears. Charges are currently rising.

Libraries need to check their requests carefully before submitting them, both to save time for the BLDSC and to prove that the item actually exists. Book requests would normally be checked in bibliographies such as the *British National Bibliography* (BNB), *Bookbank* or *United Kingdom Official Publications*, while serials requests may be checked in publications such as the *British Humanities Index* or *Abstracts in New Technologies and Engineering* (formerly *Current Technology Index*). It is usual to include a source of information with the details of your request.

The existence of the Unity catalogue and online suppliers such as Amazon have made the checking of requests very much less time consuming than it used to be.

For book requests, you need to include author, title, place of publication, year of publication, edition and ISBN or BNB number, while for periodical requests you need the serial title, year, volume number and part, together with the page references, author and title of the article and, where possible, the ISSN (International Standard Serial Number). The type of search required and acceptable formats may also be indicated.

The practical procedures involved in borrowing from and lending to other libraries have already been dealt with. As with Regional Library Bureaux, lending to and borrowing from the BLDSC requires precise recording procedures and a rigorous checking system on items that have failed to appear.

It is clear that the costs of BL loans plus the cost of the staff time involved is quite heavy, and the extent to which the costs of a BL loan are passed on to the individual requester varies from institution to institution.

Lending through the BLDSC

When lending through the BLDSC, the procedures are similar to those involved in supplying a regional interlibrary loan, although it is possible that the item will have to be sent by post; the BLDSC does send material via the transport schemes in the regions of England, but Scotland, Ireland and Wales do not have transport schemes. Again, statistics must be kept.

Common standards for good practice in interlibrary lending can be found at www.thenortheast.com/conarls.illstand.pdf.

Co-operative cataloguing

In the context of library co-operation we should also mention co-operative cataloguing in the form of the *British National Bibliography*, with its fully catalogued and classified entries and its development of MARC (MAchine Readable Cataloguing) records.

Exchange and gift schemes

There is a variety of informal schemes whereby libraries in the same locality, or libraries with similar subject coverage, exchange or donate material (although Booknet, a service run by BLDSC, has now ceased).

The best known gift scheme is Book Aid International (formerly the Ranfurly Library Service). This charity has been addressing the problem of the very poor provision of English language books in the developing world for the past 40 years, since the late Lady Ranfurly, the charity's founder and wife of the Governor-General of the Bahamas, was inspired to take action by her experiences of the appalling dearth of English books in Bahamian schools and libraries. The charity now operates in more than 70 countries, but concentrates on Africa. More than one and a half million books are donated each year to Book Aid International, by individuals, libraries and publishers. In addition, BAI buys books, encourages local publishing and trains local staff. In short, it makes a major contribution to the information needs of developing countries (see Chapter 8).

Before we leave formal library co-operation schemes, we should mention an excellent management co-operative in the south west of the

UK, Foursite, covering Bath and north east Somerset, north Somerset, Somerset and south Gloucestershire, handling joint computer systems, joint stock purchase and a joint catalogue.

Informal co-operation

Libraries and information units have a long history of informal co-operation, outside the formal structures of the Regional Bureaux and the BLDSC, and usually distinguished from formal co-operation in that normally no fixed financial transaction takes place.

This valuable informal co-operation can operate in many different ways. It can take place between libraries close in subject provision (for example, the libraries of art colleges), between libraries close in geographical location (for example, the libraries of neighbouring counties) and between libraries with similar readerships.

There is some evidence that the climate for free and informal co-operation has changed in recent years, owing, in the case of public libraries, to increasing financial constraints and in the case of academic libraries, particularly college libraries, to incorporation, which has established colleges as businesses that view neighbouring colleges as competitors in the same market rather than collaborators in the same enterprise. There has also been, particularly in academic establishments, a recent tightening of security, which often requires people to carry identification and which makes informal use of the library by outsiders more difficult.

However, informal co-operation still flourishes in a number of areas. Books may be lent informally between co-operating libraries of any of the three types listed above. Periodical articles may be supplied, and libraries may collaborate informally on the purchase and retention of serials, avoiding unnecessary duplication in specialist areas. There may be co-operation in the answering of reference enquiries, and willingness to make available any special staff expertise to other libraries. Most libraries allow free reference use to the members of other libraries, and some still allow members of other libraries to borrow, although this is not always free. There may be useful co-operative staff training ventures, particularly, for example, in the field of information technology and co-operative purchasing. A group of libraries may decide jointly to investigate a new computerized library system: they may jointly employ a computer consultant to advise, decide jointly to purchase a new system (with considerable financial savings to all the participating libraries) and may set up joint training programmes for their staff.

Free and full co-operation may have become more difficult in the present climate, but co-operative and helpful relationships between libraries remain an important feature, benefiting the services concerned, the staff and, above all, the user.

Reference

Kenyon, F. G. (1927) Great Britain, Board of Education, Public Libraries Committee, *Report on Public Libraries in England and Wales*, London, HMSO.

4 The stock of libraries

Types/range of stock

Although the term 'library' indicates a collection of books, the stock of a 21st-century library encompasses a very wide range of possible media which might include:

Abstracts
Audiotapes
Bibliographies
Books
Catalogues
College archives
Company reports
Computer-assisted learning
  packages
Computer programs
Conference proceedings
Directories
Films
Government papers
Indexes

Journals
Maps
Microforms
Newspapers
Pamphlets
Patent specifications
Pictures
Programmed texts
Prospectuses
Records
Standard specifications
Statistics
Trade literature
Three-dimensional objects
Videotapes and discs

We may think of others, both print-based (for example, musical scores) and electronic (for example CD-ROMs and DVDs), to add to this list. There is also, of course, an increasing reliance on online sources.

Clearly the range of provision in the modern library has extended greatly during the last few decades, and this broader provision has affected management, services and staffing.

The balance of types of stock varies a great deal with different types of library or information unit and the variety of services they offer. A well-managed stock reflects as specifically as possible the needs of the user.

Public libraries

In public libraries, the stock reflects the role of the library in meeting the information, education, cultural, and leisure and recreation needs of the entire community served. We discussed in Chapter 1 possible changes in the balance of these areas as information and education increase in importance, possibly at the expense of leisure and recreation.

Nevertheless, fiction forms the bulk of public library book issues (current statistics indicate that adult fiction forms more than half of total loans) and, while it would clearly be untenable to equate fiction with light reading and non-fiction with serious or educational reading, these figures do suggest overall that a considerable percentage of public library use is recreational. We expect, therefore, that the stock of public libraries will reflect this demand and that it will include a wide selection of fiction ranging from the undemanding romance to the seminal literary text. Provision for children should reflect similar demand. The expansion of non-book provision in public libraries – largely music cassettes, CDs, videos and DVDs – also very largely meets recreational demand.

A wide range of non-fiction stock, both book and periodical, meets users' education, cultural, leisure and recreational and some information needs. With the current crisis in school library provision already discussed, public libraries are increasingly having to support the National Curriculum, particularly in their non-fiction provision. There may also be specialist provision such as local history material or music scores.

A public library fulfils its information role very largely through its reference provision. Increasingly, this involves electronic as well as printed sources as libraries expand their provision of CD-ROMs and, in particular their use of the internet, often at the expense of traditional print-based provision. Reference stocks range from the small basic collections of branch libraries to the comprehensive provision of county and city reference libraries. There is an essential core reference stock. Tim Owen, in his fourth edition of *Success at the Enquiry Desk* (2003), offers a list of key reference sources (see end of this chapter).

Reference and information stock falls into several principal types (see below). Increasingly, the reference and information needs of users are met by online sources (see Chapter 5 under Digital Reference Services).

Bibliographical material

Bibliographical sources include general bibliographies such as the *British National Bibliography*, which covers all books published in this country (it commenced issue in 1950) and includes a full catalogue entry for each, including classification number. It appears in printed (weekly, monthly, quarterly and annually), microfiche and CD-ROM formats and is available online. It is the principal national bibliography and is of immense value to library staff in answering a range of bibliographical queries, whether related to author, title or subject.

Whitaker's *Books in Print* (formerly *British Books in Print*) is an annual bibliography produced by Whitaker. The CD-ROM version of this is called *Bookbank*. It is updated monthly and is also extremely useful, though aimed slightly more at the book trade than at libraries. The weekly Whitaker publication The *Bookseller* is a useful book trade list and source of information on books and publishing in general.

The publishing of bibliographic information in electronic format, particularly online, is on the increase. As well as the CD-ROM versions of the *British National Bibliography* and Whitaker's *BIP* we have bibliographies online, and library staff increasingly find themselves using online commercial enterprises such as Amazon as a very quick and useful way of answering bibliographical queries.

Major retrospective bibliographies may take the form of printed catalogues of large collections or may be available online, as in the free British Library Public Catalogue (http://catalogue.bl.uk/).

Another useful source of bibliographical information can be found in the reading lists issued in academic organizations to support courses.

There are bibliographic guides that provide specific information about certain types of book. For example *Sequels* enables users to check the correct sequence of series of novels.

Periodicals and journals form an increasingly important part of library stock and it is essential that there should be some means of accessing the mass of vital up-to-date information they contain. This is achieved by using indexing and abstracting services, which may be printed, on CD-ROM or online and which enable searches by subject. Indexing services provide a full citation (author and title of article, page reference in journal, whether the article is illustrated, plus the title, date, issue number and volume number of the journal – in fact everything one might need to request an interlibrary loan). An abstracting service also provides a short abstract (summary) of the article.

There are general indexing services such as the *Clover Information Index*, which covers popular British magazines, the *Clover Newspaper Index*, which covers UK broadsheet newspapers, and the *British Humanities Index*, which covers a wide range of general periodicals and includes abstracts. Indexing and abstracting services can have restricted subject coverage: for example *Chemical Abstracts*, *Abstracts in New Technologies and Engineering* (formerly the *Current Technology Index*), *ASSIA* (the *Applied Social Sciences Index and Abstracts*) and *LISA* (*Library and Information Science Abstracts*). *Art Index* (on CD-ROM) and *Design and Applied Arts Index* (printed) are other examples. Another type of index is the specific index to one newspaper, such as *The Times Index* and the *Financial Times Index*. Many indexing and abstracting services now appear online.

Finally in this discussion of bibliographic reference sources we turn to guides to periodicals: for example *Willing's Press Guide*, *Benn's Media Directory* and *Ulrich's International Periodicals Directory*. These enable one to check the details of periodical publications throughout the world.

Directories, yearbooks and almanacs

We now consider a group of very similar reference books. A directory is defined by Prytherch (1995) in *Harrod's Librarians' Glossary* as:

> a book containing lists of names of residents, organizations or business houses in a town, a group of towns or a country, in alphabetical order, and/or in order of situations in roads: or of firms in trade classifications arranged in alphabetical order: or of professional people, manufacturers or business houses in a particular trade or profession. A trade directory is a directory which is concerned with one trade or group of related trades.

This is a comprehensive definition, although we must remember that directories may now be on CD-ROM or online as well as in printed format. The reference stock of most libraries will contain: local directories, such as *Thomson's*; general business directories, such as *Kelly's Business Directory, Key British Enterprises, Kompass* or *Who Owns Whom*; specialized business directories, such as the *Electrical and Electronic*

Trades Directory; professional directories, such as the *Medical Directory*; specialist directories such as the *Directory of British Associations*; and, of course, telephone directories, which may be printed or online.

A yearbook – and there are blurred distinctions between directories and yearbooks – is defined by Prytherch (1995) as 'a volume often called an annual, containing current information of a variable nature, in brief descriptive and/or statistical form which is published once every year. Often yearbooks review the events of a year.' Many quick reference queries can be answered from yearbooks such as the *Statesman's Yearbook*, the *Municipal Yearbook*, the *Stock Exchange Official Yearbook* and the *Civil Service Yearbook*.

It is often difficult to distinguish between a yearbook and an almanac, which is described by Prytherch (1995) as 'a publication, usually an annual, containing a variety of useful facts of a miscellaneous nature, and statistical information'. Having come a long way from their early links with astrological information and predictions, almanacs are an extremely useful reference source and *Whitaker's Almanack* has been described with justification as the single most significant and useful reference source for library and information staff.

Encyclopedias

All reference stocks contain encyclopedias, the staple providers of a vast range of easily accessible knowledge. They come in a variety of types, and increasingly are on CD-ROM as well as in printed format, with the former, in some cases, incorporating sound and moving images as well as text. Increasingly, encyclopedias are available online.

There are general one-volume encyclopedias such as *Pears Cyclopaedia*, general multi-volume encyclopedias such as *World Book Encyclopaedia* and *Encyclopaedia Britannica*, and specialized encyclopedias such as the *McGraw-Hill Encyclopaedia of Science and Technology*, the *Dictionary of Art* and *Grove's Dictionary of Music and Musicians* (these last two are in fact encyclopedias, though they are called dictionaries).

Encyclopedias should be authoritative (signed articles are a good indicator), frequently updated, comprehensive and unbiased. Their arrangement should be logical, and the index full. It is useful if the articles contain bibliographies and illustrations. The level should be appropriate to the client group – for example, it would be inappropriate for a primary school library to stock *Encyclopaedia Britannica*.

Dictionaries

Libraries and information units need to stock a wide range of dictionaries. A dictionary is basically an alphabetical list of words with their meanings and usually various other items of information. They can range from general dictionaries such as *The Concise Oxford Dictionary of Current English*, to specialist dictionaries such as the *Penguin Dictionary of Mathematics*, through dictionaries that are really specialist encyclopaedias, such as *Grove's Dictionary of Music and Musicians*, to bilingual dictionaries such as *Cassell's English–Spanish Spanish–English Dictionary*.

We must also consider dictionaries of synonyms, such as *Roget's Thesaurus*, of abbreviations, such as *The Oxford Dictionary of Abbreviations*, of etymology, such as *The Oxford Dictionary of English Etymology*, of slang, such as *Partridge's Dictionary of Slang and Unconventional English*, and of phrases and sayings, such as *Brewer's Dictionary of Phrase and Fable*. As with other major reference sources, many dictionaries are now available online.

Business information

Any reference library or information unit that serves a business or commercial community must provide trade literature, and standards and patent information. Trade literature is usually defined as product literature, that is, promotional literature produced by commercial organizations, often about specific products. It is more widely used in commercial and special libraries than in public libraries. Trade literature has the great advantage of normally being free, though obviously the fact that it is specifically promotional may affect its value as an information source. We must also consider in this context packaged services, such as the *Building Product Microfile* and the *Health and Safety Microfile*, which are both produced by Barbour Index plc.

British Standards are produced by the British Standards Institution (BSI), the approved body for the preparation and promulgation of national standards. The BSI was the first national standards body in the world: it covers standards in building and civil engineering, materials and chemicals, engineering, electrotechnology, consumer products and services, healthcare, management systems and information technology. The BSI *Standards Catalogue* is issued annually, and the standards themselves are available online.

A patent is defined by Prytherch (1995) as 'a specification concerning the designs or manufacture of something which is protected by letters patent and secured for the exclusive profit of the designer or inventor for a limited number of years'. Collections of patents are held at large commercial libraries and at the British Library

Quotation sources and concordances

A further group of reference sources is formed by quotation sources and concordances, of which there are a number. Perhaps the most famous is *Stevenson's Book of Quotations*, sadly now out of print. New editions of *The Oxford Dictionary of Quotations* and Bartlett's *Familiar Quotations* are available, as are the best known of the concordances, *Cruden's Complete Concordance to the Old and New Testament* and *Bartlett's Complete Concordance to the Works of Shakespeare*.

Biographical sources

Biographical reference sources form a very important part of reference stock. The general encyclopaedias we have already discussed can form a very useful source of biographical information, especially for figures from the past, as can specific encyclopaedias such as *The Cambridge Biographical Encyclopaedia*. The major source for British retrospective biographical information is the *Dictionary of National Biography*. The updated *New Dictionary of National Biography* appeared in book and electronic form in 2004.

Current and recent biographical information can be found in *Current Biography*, *Who's Who*, *International Who's Who* and *Who Was Who*.

Geographical and travel information

Reference collections need a wide range of geographical sources in the form of maps, atlases and gazetteers, ranging from the various Ordnance Survey series (Explorer, Landranger, Outdoor Leisure), through specialist atlases, such as motoring atlases, to major world atlases such as the *Times Atlas of the World* and *Philips' Great World Atlas*. Gazetteers often accompany atlases and are described by Prytherch (1995) as 'geographical dictionaries with a varying amount of descriptive, geographical, historical or statistical information'.

We turn finally to timetables. Many quick reference queries may be answered from the major bus, coach, train, air, cruise and ferry timetables, some of which, such as the national rail passenger timetables, are also available on CD-ROM. Many are also available on the internet.

Academic libraries

The stock of academic libraries – schools, colleges and universities – usually offers a different balance. A much higher proportion of non-fiction reflects the need for stock to support the courses being taught, both specifically in narrow curriculum terms and in a more general cultural context.

Academic libraries are also likely to have a larger reference stock, short-loan facilities and a much wider range of media, which is likely to include a considerable periodical and journal stock (this is particularly true of college and university libraries), a range of audiovisual stock, such as slides and cassettes, and electronic provision, such as CD-ROMs, computer programs and access to the internet. School libraries may provide topic packs, either commercially produced or put together by library staff, to support the various areas of the National Curriculum.

The needs of the academic library user differ from those of the general user of a public library in that they are largely though not entirely educational rather than recreational, and the stock provided clearly reflects these differing needs. The balance between the use of printed and electronic reference sources in academic libraries is shifting, with greatly increasing reliance on electronic sources, particularly on the internet.

Special libraries

The role of special libraries and information units or workplace libraries, which is to support the needs of a very limited clientèle in order to improve the efficiency of the organization, is reflected in a stock that will have a very limited and specific focus, may be entirely for reference only and will contain a very high proportion of journals, reports, monographs and learned papers because of the prime necessity of material being entirely up to date. Such libraries will certainly have internet and online facilities.

Selecting, ordering and processing stock

Selecting stock for a library is one of the most rewarding aspects of a librarian's work. In most libraries it is seen as part of the role of professional staff, though it is becoming increasingly acknowledged that paraprofessional staff, with their close awareness of user demand, have a vital part to play here. In academic libraries this is often a conflict area, with little agreement as to the respective roles of library staff and teaching/lecturing staff in the selection of stock.

Subject to the normal restraints of finance and space, it is the job of a library to meet the perceived needs of all of its users. Factors to be taken into consideration in stock selection include the necessity of maintaining a balanced stock related specifically to the changing needs of the community served, the need to be up to date, the need to fulfil any subject specialization requirements and the need to fulfil specific user requests. Public libraries need to be alert to changes in the community profile, for example changes in ethnic balance, while academic libraries need to respond to changes in courses and curricula, and to supply required texts and background material.

There are various ways in which library staff ensure they are aware of current publishing output:

1 They may visit local bookshops, library suppliers and specialist suppliers.
2 They will regularly read general publications such as *The Bookseller* and the *British National Bibliography*. Other useful sources include publishers' catalogues, suppliers' publicity material, and critical and evaluative articles in publications such as the serious newspapers, *The Times Literary Supplement*, *The School Librarian* and *Books for Keeps*.
3 Some library suppliers send approval collections of books to selection meetings held by senior staff.

For non-print stock there are sources such as the *British Catalogue of Audiovisual Materials*. There are various specialist journals such as *BBC Music Magazine*, *Gramophone* and the *Classic FM Magazine*, which help in the selection of music CDs, while companies such as Visual Publications issue regular catalogues of slides. Videos of an educational nature are covered by catalogues such as those issued by BBC Education or Educational Film Services, while videos intended for entertainment are normally covered in general magazines, newspapers and specialist journals such as *Which Video*.

Sources of supply

Once appropriate stock has been selected, the next step is to determine appropriate sources of supply.

Although the collapse of the Net Book Agreement in 1995 had a damaging effect on small booksellers, as large booksellers and even supermarkets now sell large quantities of discounted stock, the effect on library purchasing does not appear to have been as damaging as was originally feared. In fact, libraries have often been able to negotiate discounts larger than 10% from the increasingly competitive library suppliers, and have also been able to negotiate very economically advantageous terms for processing to be done by the supplier. Small libraries which cannot command large discounts from suppliers because of their low level of spending are beginning to join consortia. These groups, such as the Foursite Consortium (Somerset, south Gloucestershire, north Somerset and Bath and north east Somerset), will combine the spending power within a sector or a region and will be able to negotiate higher discounts from library suppliers for their members. In fact, deregulation of the market has to some extent benefited libraries: it is the number of library suppliers that may not be sustained as profits fall.

The usual options for stock purchase are as follows:

1 Local retail booksellers: although books may be ordered through local retail outlets, local booksellers are particularly useful for shelfpicks, that is, a visit from library staff to choose directly from the shelves. Sometimes, however, it can be difficult for local booksellers to accommodate the special nature of local authority financial arrangements!

2 Specialist booksellers: there are many shops that cater for well-defined specific subject needs with a far greater range of stock than might be found in a general supplier – for example, the Building Bookshop, or the bookshops attached to art galleries such as the Arnolfini in Bristol, or the National and Tate Galleries and the Royal Academy in London. There are also specialist suppliers of non-book material.

3 Traditional library suppliers: these are firms that specialize in selling to libraries and other institutions. They will generally hold a large volume of stock across a wide subject range, and will be able to acquire material quickly from publishers if it is not in stock. As well as a discount and processing facilities, library suppliers also offer services such as an on-approval scheme, catalogues, regular visits from a representative, publicity and display material such as dustjackets, bibliographical

checking, standing order facilities for reference material and regular financial statements.

Periodicals are acquired rather differently, either directly from the publisher, through a subscription agent such as Blackwells or through a local newsagent.

Manual ordering procedures

After stock has been chosen and the appropriate supplier decided upon, items are ordered. It is essential to have a series of procedures in place to ensure the smooth transition from ordering to shelf. Libraries normally keep an alphabetical file of suppliers, with details of their services. Depending on the library/information unit and its ordering system, these procedures may be manual, computerized or a combination of both.

Organizations that still use manual ordering systems – which can be very reliable but slow – usually make use of pre-printed stationery to build up an order file. An order slip is prepared for each title to be ordered, containing information describing the item (author, title, publisher, date, price, ISBN), information concerning the order and supplier (number of copies, name of supplier, date of order, official order number, any reports) and information for library use on receipt of the item (name of requester, which cost centre, eventual location of material). These slips are often produced in duplicate or triplicate form if a copy of this information is required by more than one person. Before the information on one of these slips is transferred to the official order it should be checked against the library catalogue to ensure that the item is not already in stock, and against the on-order file to ensure that it is not already on order.

The official order should then be created which, as well as the details of the items required, should contain the name and address of the library and specific delivery point if necessary, the official order number and date, the cost of each item and the total cost of the order, the authorized signature and the name and address of the supplier. Official orders are often produced in triplicate, one copy going to the supplier, one to the library's administrative and financial centre, and the third retained by the library and filed in order number sequence.

Once the information on the order slip has been transferred to the official order the order slip may be filed alphabetically in the on-order file: this file is vital as it enables the library to identify quickly which items are on order, for and from whom the item has been ordered, and the progress of the order.

Computerized ordering is faster, simpler and more efficient, and is taking over from manual ordering.

Receiving new stock

Unpacking new stock, particularly new books, is one of the most enjoyable parts of working in a library or information unit, particularly for those who have been drawn to library work by a passion for books!

The procedures involved in receiving new stock must be systematic. The address on the delivery must be checked to ensure that the parcel has come to the correct place, and the contents of the parcel must be checked against the delivery note to ensure everything is as it should be.

In the case of books, these must be sorted into alphabetical order and each title matched with the appropriate order slip, which should be withdrawn from the on-order file. Each book should be inspected for defects. Titles should then be checked against the invoice (which is either in the parcel or will be sent separately) and the official order, both of which should be marked up as necessary. When the financial details on the invoice have been checked as correct, payment may be authorized and the invoice passed to the finance department, the library copy of the official order having been marked to indicate that the order has arrived. A copy of the invoice should be filed in the copy invoice file in case there are any subsequent queries. Any material that is incorrect or damaged should be returned to the supplier and a credit note requested.

There need to be in place other precise procedures to deal with, for example, chasing overdue items, inspection copies, standing orders and cancelled orders.

Periodicals

The ordering and receipt of periodicals follow a very different procedure. The receipt of periodicals is regulated, in theory, by issue dates, although in practice these can be very erratic. It is vital that libraries keep accurate records and promptly chase missing issues of a subscription, as an issue can go out of print very quickly, making it difficult to maintain a complete run. The usual manual means of indicating the arrival of individual issues is to use some sort of visible index. This may be time consuming and laborious but, operated meticulously, can be very dependable. Each card in the visible index displays the title of the journal, together with publisher, price, frequency of publication, date of arrival, subscription details, order number and details of binding, location and storage.

Computerized ordering procedures

As can be seen from the above description, manual ordering and receipt procedures for both book and non-book materials are indeed repetitive and very time consuming, and are therefore ideal for computerization.

Ordering packages are often known within automated systems as acquisition modules. These packages do not perform tasks that a manual system cannot perform, but they can perform with far greater speed. The added advantage is that automated systems will only require data entry for each title once, and if this is at the ordering stage then it will save time later at the cataloguing and circulation stages, when the same data can be transferred through the system and added to appropriately. The use of computerized ordering has greatly increased in recent years. Many library suppliers, such as Dawsons, combine online ordering facilities with the provision of bibliographical information.

Computerized systems automatically produce orders based on specific order numbers: any item on order can be displayed on screen together with its current progress. Reports on delayed items may be generated automatically.

Computerized ordering systems for periodicals are called serials packages or modules, and again perform the same functions as a manual process but with greater speed. Entry of each title may take some time, but once this has taken place the system will generate lists of missed issues and automatic renewal forms.

We must also mention online ordering through companies such as Amazon.

Processing

The next step in the progress of an item from selection, through ordering and receipt, to appearing on the shelves, is processing. As has been mentioned, it is very likely that processing will largely be carried out by the suppliers, who, for commercial reasons, have taken over what used to be a significant part of the duties of a library or information assistant.

Processing of books consists of accessioning (assigning a unique number), putting on a plastic jacket to extend life, inserting appropriate stationery (date label and barcode for computerized systems; date label, book pocket and book card for manual issue systems such as Browne), inserting appropriate security devices, stamping with the library stamp and, after classification, attaching a spinal label.

Precision and accuracy are essential in the processing of books and indeed of all library material.

Arranging and accessing stock

When the public library movement, with its major lending function, got underway in the 19th century, it soon became obvious that finding ways to arrange stock most effectively to reflect the demands of users was a very important issue. The pre-19th-century libraries with their minimal lending function could arrange their stock in a number of ways: by date, by author or by shelfmark. As the provision of public libraries gathered momentum it became clear that the demand, outside fiction which was primarily arranged by author, was for arrangement by subject. In other words, most non-fiction books are read because of their subject matter irrespective of publisher, title, colour, size and often author. Thus the 19th and early 20th centuries saw the development of the great subject classification schemes, most of which are in use today.

Subject classification schemes

Most of the development of classification schemes took place in the USA. Bliss's Bibliographic Classification was created at the beginning of the 20th century by H. E. Bliss, librarian at the College of the City of New York. This full and scholarly scheme has been, and in fact is still being, radically revised and is still in use today, mainly in academic and educational libraries.

Also still in use today, but initially devised just before Bliss, is the Library of Congress Classification, which was developed to meet the needs of that library's vast stock and which was partly based on Dewey. Another contemporary scheme still very widely used today is the Universal Decimal Classification (UDC), which is really an expansion of Dewey and which is constantly being revised and updated.

The Colon Classification, devised in the 1930s by the noted Indian scholar S. R. Ranganathan, is a complex and impressive scheme – perhaps more impressive in theory than in practice.

However, we would like to focus in our discussion of classification on the Dewey Decimal Classification (DDC), initially devised by Melvil Dewey in 1873, constantly updated and now available on CD-ROM and online. Not only is it the most widely used, practical and familiar scheme, especially in public libraries, but it also provides an appropriate context in which to discuss classification theory and practice.

Classification issues

In general terms, classification is something we do all the time in everyday life: it is the means by which we bring similar things together and separate dissimilar things. It is a complex and profound activity springing from our view of the world in general. Classification in libraries has many organizational advantages apart from the obvious one of reflecting the way in which users seek material.

In most schemes the order itself is helpful, showing the main relationships between subjects. It is clear that in assigning a classification number to an item we are making certain decisions not only about its subject, but also about the relationship of that subject to other subjects. Let us suppose that we have in front of us a book entitled *Nineteenth Century Italian Ceramics*. Are its closest links with 20th-century Italian ceramics, with 19th-century Italian sculpture or with 19th-century French ceramics – in other words, where are the relationships strongest, between countries, between art forms or between periods? A published classification scheme will have made these decisions and given appropriate guidance.

Classifying material for a library consistently and correctly requires a knowledge of classification theory. A layperson's view that all that is required is to look up a number in an index could not be further from the truth – it is in fact only too easy to recognize a library that has been classified without an adequate knowledge of classification theory! We will discuss the process of classifying later.

Reshelving of returned material is made easier by the presence of the spinal label bearing the classification number, reference from catalogue entry to material is easy, as is shelfguiding, stocktaking and the keeping of statistics: such are the benefits of library classification. However, there are some inevitable disadvantages to library classification schemes. First, it is impossible to arrange material on the shelves so that every relationship is shown; when we discuss cataloguing, we will explore the means by which a catalogue may help with this. Second, most classification schemes were begun in the 19th century. Since then the order of knowledge has changed. Who now would think of putting psychology with philosophy, as Dewey did? Similarly, some areas of knowledge, most particularly in technology, have expanded rapidly, while others have remained relatively static, thus distorting the original scheme. Third, high staffing levels are needed to maintain the strict order on the shelves that is necessary for the efficient use of a classified stock, and very heavy workloads are involved if large areas of stock need reclassifying.

The content of a classification scheme

Of what does a classification scheme consist, and what are the desirable qualities of its constituent parts?

Schedules

The main bulk of any scheme is the schedules. Schedules are the printed lists of all the main classes, divisions and subdivisions of the classification scheme, the arrangement being logical and hierarchical in that it shows the relationships of specific subjects to parent subjects; also shown is the classification notation. Dewey, for example, divides knowledge into ten main classes: each class has ten divisions, each division ten subdivisions, and so on. Schedules need to be full, logical, accurate and expressive of relationships.

Notation

Notation is the system of symbols used to express the classification scheme. A notation may be pure – that is, it may consist of one type of symbol only (Dewey uses a pure numerical notation: for example, medicine is indicated by the number 610) – or it may be mixed and use both letters and numbers. Dewey's use of a decimalized numerical notation has many advantages: numbers are clear, easy to remember, offer scope for mnemonic devices (for example, it is an aid to memory if the same numbers have the same meaning across large areas of the scheme) and, above all, the notation is infinitely expandable to deal with new areas of knowledge. There may be very long notations, with many digits after the decimal points – for example, some classification numbers in relatively new areas of knowledge, such as some aspects of television engineering, may be very long (621.3883320288 is the maintenance and repair of video recordings) – but any new subject may be accommodated. Numerical notations are easy to use in computerized systems and can be applied to a range of media other than books.

The index

A classification scheme also needs a detailed index. An index is an alphabetical list of those subjects covered by the scheme, together with the appropriate classification number. In the case of Dewey, what we have is a relative index. A relative index includes, indented below the subject term, the various contexts/aspects of that subject. For example, if we looked up 'Guns' in the Dewey relative index, we would find a range of contexts indented below: art metalwork, manufacturing technology, military engineering, sports and so on. The index to a classification scheme should be full, detailed and accurate.

Tables

The final feature of a classification scheme is the tables, which are additional to the schedules, may be added to classification numbers right across the scheme as directed by the schedules, and make the final class mark even more specific and precise. For example, in Dewey, where there is a wide range of tables, the table of form divisions enables you to denote treatment of subject. For example, 03 denotes dictionary when added to a subject number from the schedules, so that if 610 = medicine, 610.3 = a dictionary of medicine.

The process of classification

The act of classifying is precise, time-consuming and far from straightforward. We have carried out experiments with students and found that with more complex material it is quite possible for a class of 20 library assistants to come up with 20 differing classification numbers, of which perhaps three would be possibilities.

A thorough look at the item to be classified – if a book, the blurb on the dustjacket and the qualifications of the author are helpful indications, as is a brief look at the contents – is the first step. Once the precise subject has been decided, the most appropriate term should be looked up in the relative index. This will lead the classifier to the schedules to seek the most appropriate classmark and then, if appropriate, to the tables to make the classmark even more specific and precise. Only then is it appropriate to check to see what previous decisions have been made for similar items. Obviously if this were done first, original mistakes would be perpetuated. However, where more than one decision is possible, earlier decisions must have an influence for the sake of consistency.

Classification within library and information work is currently the subject of much discussion. It has always been seen as part of the responsibilities of a qualified librarian because of the need for a knowledge of classification theory although, increasingly, paraprofessional staff may undertake some aspects, particularly when small collections of discrete material such as pamphlets are involved or classification is very broad (that is, using short class number as in school libraries). The fact that the *British National Bibliography* gives Dewey numbers may also be useful for the inexperienced or unqualified classifier.

Most library and information units adapt the classification scheme to their own particular needs. For example, public libraries usually remove fiction from its place in the classification scheme and arrange it by author surname. This is done because it reflects normal user demand. However, a decision like this is not without its problems. Dewey, for example, would separate novels by Charles Dickens from books about the novels of Charles Dickens, which would be classified within the literature class (800). 'Broken order' refers to this practice of removing sections of stock from a classified sequence and arranging it by some other criterion. 'Parallel arrangements', on the other hand, refer to the practice of moving, for example, oversize books or reference books from the main classified sequence to another sequence, but one which also follows the same classification scheme.

Stock categorization

As we have said, subject classification schemes were developed because arranging material by specific subject reflected user demand far more fully than arranging material by any of the other possible criteria, such as size, date of publication, date of purchase, publisher, colour, shelfmark or title. Most libraries and information units continue to arrange in classified order, but during recent years there has been a tendency in public libraries to consider stock categorization as a possible alternative.

Stock categorization can be applied in three ways. As applied to fiction, it involves choosing categories, such as crime, historical, science fiction and so on, and arranging fiction books within these categories. Practice differs – the categorization may be very casual and the category chosen depend on the individual shelver (a recipe for disaster!), or a novel may be categorized at the time of cataloguing, and its category appear both in the catalogue entry and on the spine of the item. Within each category, arrangement may be random, or alphabetical by author.

There are advantages and disadvantages to the categorization of fiction. For library users, choice may be easier, but exploratory or developmental reading is not encouraged. For library staff, depending on the way in which categorization is put into practice, shelving may be quicker, and stock shortages in certain categories of stock easier to spot, but finding individual requests may be difficult, and if choice of category is left to individual assistants all sorts of anomalies may occur.

The categorization of non-fiction is a more controversial procedure and less commonly applied. It is a response to the fact that, while a specific subject-based classified arrangement does reflect major need, it does not help the general non-fiction reader, who may be more interested in a general topic rather than a specific subject. It involves selecting broad topic areas such as leisure, travel and hobbies, rather in the manner of a bookshop, and arranging material under these categories. It is important to note that a choice needs to be made here – stock can be arranged either by specific subject or by broad topic – and there are numerous organizational implications (how to trace specific items, what to put in the catalogue or on the item and so on). Categorization of non-fiction stock has normally been applied only to small service points such as mobile libraries.

However, categorization may be applied in other areas of a library without controversy. For example, categorization by age of intended reader may be used to organize material for children, compact discs may be categorized as classical, folk, jazz and so on, and categorization frequently occurs on a temporary basis with the pulling together of materials relevant to a topic of current interest for display purposes.

Cataloguing

We now turn to cataloguing, an area of library and information work that has undergone vast changes in the last 20 years.

A catalogue is a list, arranged in a recognizable order, containing certain information. Before the advent of computerized cataloguing, there were various physical forms of catalogue: printed, guardbook, sheaf and microform, for example. However, the most widely used physical form of catalogue was the card catalogue, of which many examples are still in use today. A card catalogue normally consists of:

- a classified catalogue, in which the catalogue cards are arranged in order of their classification number
- an author/title catalogue, in which the author cards are arranged alphabetically by author surname and are interspersed with title cards, where appropriate, arranged alphabetically under the first word of the title
- a subject index consisting of subject headings and their classification numbers.

Thus items could be traced if the author, title or classification number were known.

Consistent and accurate cataloguing rules have to be followed if an efficient manual catalogue is to be maintained, in order to provide a clear, consistent and efficient route to the shelves for both readers and library staff. The most widely used code of cataloguing rules was, and still is, the *Anglo-American Cataloguing Rules* (1988), usually referred to as *AACR2*. This is the cataloguers' bible – nearly 700 pages long, detailed, complex and comprehensive, including within it new developments, such as the increasing need to include non-book materials, and the spread of computerized and centralized cataloguing.

Manual cataloguing

Traditionally (though the approach may be modified in computerized cataloguing), the main catalogue entry for an item will be made up of five main parts:

- the heading (usually the author's surname)
- the title
- the imprint (place of publication, name of publisher and date of publication)
- the collation (physical description)
- notes.

With the advent of computerized cataloguing, and in particular its ability to use a wider range of keywords in a search, issues such as the correct choice of heading are no longer so vital. There are very precise rules to be followed concerning the filing of catalogue cards, spelling out in detail how to deal with a vast range of possibilities in areas such as, for example, surnames with prefixes, abbreviations, the same word used as author and title, numbers, hyphenated words and so on. Most cataloguers and filers used the American Library Association filing code to ensure consistency and correct practice. It is difficult now when we are all used to computerized catalogues to realize how easily an item could be lost in a catalogue if correct procedures were not adhered to.

The actual method of filing – word by word or letter by letter – had also to be decided upon and followed consistently.

Indexing, used to compile the subject index so vital to the efficient use of a manual catalogue, was also subject to full and complex rules, but has become less significant with the advent of computerized cataloguing.

Throughout the period when manual (mainly card) catalogues were the norm, the *British National Bibliography* contained full catalogue entries for every item it contained, which was a helpful form of centralized cataloguing available for those who wished to use it. Cataloguers could either use the *BNB* as a guide in cases of difficulty, or purchase *BNB* printed catalogue cards for insertion into library catalogues.

Computerized cataloguing

We now turn to computerized cataloguing, the development that above all others has revolutionized library and information sector practice.

There is a variety of library computerized systems on the market. Basically they take over the library housekeeping systems and the catalogue. Cataloguing becomes in effect data input. OPACs (computerized catalogues for public use) have great advantages over the old-fashioned card catalogue. In a good system, they are user-friendly for even the most nervous user, and difficult to damage. They can tell you if an item is out on loan and, if so, when it is due for return. Some organizations, particularly university libraries, allow users to access their own records through the OPACs, and renew and reserve material themselves. Perhaps the biggest benefit of computerized catalogues is the multiplicity of search routes, so the choice of heading is less vital. On most systems you may search by author, title, classification number and keyword. This keyword facility, which, unless it is limited to keyword in title only, depends on the cataloguer's having added appropriate subject keywords into the keyword field at the time of data input, has greatly increased the likelihood of matching user with required subject and thus has enabled the stock to be much more fully exploited than was previusly possible. In the time of manual catalogues, matching user and subject all too often depended on the subject knowledge of library staff.

Computerized cataloguing has brought the need for new skills in library staff: the need for computer literacy, to understand keywording, and to develop and teach new and precise research and information retrieval techniques. It has also led to the development of standards for the exchange of bibliographical data in machine-readable form (the MARC format). Centralized cataloguing has been enabled by the development of computerized systems from which member libraries can call up existing records instead of having to catalogue from scratch. In recent years, almost all libraries have gone over to computerized cataloguing, and it is clear that manual cataloguing may soon be a thing of the past.

Managing stock 1 – stock control, circulation control and issue systems
Stock control

It is a basic function of all types of library or information unit that an individual item can be located (via the catalogue and the issue system), found (via an appropriate shelving system, usually by classification number), lent where appropriate (through an efficient issue system), returned (again through the issue system) and reshelved (via the shelving arrangement). The means to do this is known as stock control. Any method of stock control that does not enable us to carry out these functions quickly and with maximum efficiency is failing as a system.

An additional and essential feature of stock control is stock monitoring. This can be carried out in various ways: its purpose is to ensure that the library or information unit is meeting the developing or changing needs of its users as fully and specifically as possible. The obvious method is the keeping of issue statistics which, even in their simplest form, can give us information about how heavily stock is used and at what periods the use is heaviest. If a computerized issue system is in use it is possible to monitor stock usage by subject, and also to check the loan history of particular items: in a manual system, date labels will be checked for indication of usage, though obviously this does not help with reference use. Foot counts can also be a means of monitoring the use of a library or information unit.

Circulation control and issue systems

We have already dealt with the first two elements of stock control – that is, the ability to locate items through a catalogue and find them through the arrangement on the shelves. We now turn to circulation control, a vital element of stock control that embraces all the procedures connected with the lending function: the registration of users, the issue, discharge and reservation of library materials, and the recording and keeping of issue statistics. Circulation control is another area in the library and information sector that has been revolutionized by computerization.

Any issue system needs to be able to answer a list of questions. Is a certain item out? When is it due for return? Who has it on loan? How many items does a certain user have on loan? Have overdues been sent? Are fines payable? Is the item reserved for another reader? It should be capable of dealing accurately and speedily with heavy usage, and have minimal potential for human error. Since the early days of the public library movement, many different issue systems have been tried with varying degrees of success, ranging from self-issue to photocharging, from Browne to computerized issue.

The most popular and efficient manual system, which is still in use today, is the Browne system. This involves a user being given one ticket per loan entitlement, and each item for loan being given a book card within a book pocket. When the loan takes place, the book card is placed into the user ticket (this now becomes known as the charge) and the charge is filed in trays behind date guides in whatever order (author, accession number) is deemed appropriate. Although perfectly adequate if managed properly, Browne is very time-consuming in terms of routine procedures such as overdues and reservations, and tends to reduce library counter staff to filing clerks.

The wide range of computerized issue systems now available as part of library computer systems is based on barcodes on the user's library card and the item for loan: an issue is effected by scanning both barcodes with a light pen or other device. Computerized systems, although not immune from human error, are fast and efficient, and capable of a far more sophisticated approach in terms of categories of reader, categories of material, and detailed and complex statistics. A major development now gathering pace is the provision of computerized self-issue systems, particularly in university libraries.

Managing stock 2 – security measures

A significant factor in the management of stock on open access to users is the prevention of loss. In the days before the development of public and academic library services into their current roles, stock in libraries was normally on closed access – that is, not directly available to the public. This meant that when borrowing was permitted it was through the library staff: users consulted a catalogue in order to choose books, which were then fetched by staff. This system had many disadvantages – for example, it prevented any browsing of stock by borrowers – but it certainly reduced to a minimum the possibility of theft. The development of open-access services brought with it problems in terms of the safety of stock from theft and loss.

It is obviously both demoralizing for library staff and detrimental to the service if the items that have been so carefully selected, ordered, classified, catalogued and processed should then be lost or stolen, thus unbalancing the stock and representing a serious financial loss. The Library and Information Statistics Unit at Loughborough University estimates the average annual book loss from public libraries in the UK at approximately 4% of stock. In many libraries, both public and academic, it is considerably higher, sometimes as much as 10%.

Minimizing loss

Libraries can take many sensible steps to minimize levels of loss. The design of both the building and the interior layout should make it difficult to remove material illegally. Entrances and exits should be clearly visible to staff, and well signed. All doors and windows, especially those in closed areas such as toilets, should be protected to stop material being passed out of the library. The stock itself should be well marked and labelled to deter those whose intention it is to steal and sell material on to the second-hand book trade, and also to make it easier to challenge anyone suspected of removing material illegally. Photocopying facilities should be provided at reasonable cost to prevent in particular the theft of periodicals.

Enrolment and induction procedures should encourage people to join the library and borrow material legally and responsibly, making it unnecessary for them to resort to illegal means. Circulation policies should be appropriate to the needs of borrowers, enabling them to borrow what they need for an appropriate loan period, without excessive overdue charges, thus making it unnecessary for them to bypass the legal borrowing procedures.

It is a good idea for staff to be aware of areas where losses are most likely to occur and to keep a special watch on them. It is often advisable to put very valuable materials and media such as CDs on closed access, in the latter case by displaying just the covers.

Library housekeeping procedures are important in both preventing and detecting losses. It is important to keep shelves tidy – in libraries using a computerized system that indicates that an item is on the shelves, not out on loan, it is particularly embarrassing if untidy shelves make it impossible to find – and to shelve returned items as quickly as possible. Strict organizational procedures should be in place to ensure that items are never removed from the shelves by library staff, for whatever reason, without an appropriate record being kept. It is very frustrating for staff and users if time is wasted searching for an item that the catalogue indicates should be on the shelves only to find that it has been removed for reclassification or repair. Regular stocktaking, if time permits, is the only accurate indicator of losses.

Many libraries, particularly academic libraries, do not allow bags and coats into the library as a strategy to minimize theft.

Security systems

The modern library, however, is likely to rely for the security of its stock on electronic security systems, of which there are a number on the market. Although there are differences in individual systems, most of them work on the principle of tagging an item with a metallic trigger – for example, in the form of a metallic strip fitted within the spine of a book – which, if not desensitized, activates an alarm at the exit gates. A machine able to desensitize and resensitize items is kept at the issue desk. When items are issued they are desensitized to enable the user to pass through the security gates without setting off the alarm system. On return the item is resensitized before shelving. Reference stock may be fitted with permanently sensitized triggers, although this can give rise to problems if reference material is ever transferred to lending stock.

Libraries and information units operate systems such as these in a variety of ways. Some choose to insert triggers into all stock, some into only a percentage of it.

Electronic security systems undoubtedly reduce losses caused by both deliberate theft and inadvertent removal very significantly, and for libraries whose stocktaking exercises reveal substantial losses they are the only sensible answer. Some years ago Somerset College of Arts and

Technology introduced a security system in response to annual losses in the order of 8–10% . Losses were reduced immediately to less than 1%! However, security systems are not without their disadvantages and problems.

Disadvantages of security systems

If library staff are not trained to respond sensitively, customer relationships may suffer. Personal experience tells us that deliberate theft is comparatively rare, and should never be assumed. Forgetfulness or confusion about the issue system is a much more likely explanation and staff reaction should reflect this – house rules should always preclude accusations of theft! When security systems were first introduced there was a genuine concern that their introduction would damage the trust between library staff and user. If proper guidelines are established this does not usually prove to be the case.

Some libraries and information units have reported increased mutilation of books and periodicals following the installation of a security system – in other words, users remove bits of the item if they are prevented from removing the whole. However, the provision of photocopiers can go a long way towards overcoming this potential problem, which in our experience has never been a major concern anyway.

All security systems to a greater or lesser extent suffer from false alarms, which can be embarrassing for the users and time-wasting for the staff. These false alarms may be caused by the proximity of computers, automated issue terminals or even by heart pacemakers, belt buckles, dental fillings or other metallic objects. Quite often the reason for a false alarm cannot be ascertained. If there is an unacceptably large number of false alarms, the power of the system may have to be reduced, which inevitably also reduces its effectiveness. A balance has to be achieved, therefore, and an acceptable level of false alarms decided upon.

Cost is a major factor, and has to be balanced against the cost of projected stock losses. The initial capital expenditure on a library security system would depend upon the number of issue points, the number of access points and the particular system purchased, but typically would be in the region of £14,000, with the annual maintenance contract running at about 10–15% of that. In addition, there is the ongoing cost of the actual triggers (about 12p per item) and either the staff time to insert them or, as is more common now, the cost of paying the stock supplier to do it. Systems may need upgrading from time to time, and this is another cost.

Any preconceived idea that staff costs may be cut by installing a security system usually turns out to have been unrealistic, although it is true that staff do not then have to carry out many duties more usually associated with security officers.

Disaster can strike if the system breaks down or there is a power cut, if the electronic security system is the only means of security in operation. Items being issued will not be desensitized and items being returned will not be resensitized. The effects of this will last well after the security system is back in action, in that not all of the shelved stock will be 'live', and will thus be unprotected, whereas some of the issued items will be, thus causing embarrassment to perfectly innocent users who will set off the alarm.

Problems may be caused, particularly in school and college libraries, if students attempt to discover how the items are protected. Most believe it is the barcode! If the magnetic device is discovered it can be used to play tricks on unsuspecting fellow students, who will inevitably set off the alarm system if they are unaware that a magnetic strip has been hidden in their bags – a time-wasting and irritating practice.

Finally, not all library material can be easily tagged, so it may not be possible to secure the entire stock. Non-book and audiovisual material may be particularly difficult. In addition, some library materials such as computer disks, video cassettes and audio cassettes may be irretrievably damaged if passed through a sensitizer.

It is clear, however, that provided the costs are efficiently balanced – it would be absurd, for example, to spend £20,000 to save £5,000 in book losses – electronic security systems represent the best way of securing stock.

Care of stock

In all types of library and information unit it is essential that every possible step is taken to care appropriately for all types of stock, not only because the current funding crises make this an essential part of good practice but because users have the right to an attractive, appropriate and cared-for stock. Therefore an appropriate and efficient system for the physical care of stock is an essential part of stock management. Paraprofessional library staff have a major responsibility here. As many of their duties – issuing, discharging, shelving and shelf tidying, for instance – bring them constantly into contact with stock, they are often in the best position to note and deal with damaged items, although the decision whether to rebind, repair or discard may well be taken by a library manager.

All types of stock need appropriate shelving/storage. Inappropriate shelving in terms of size can damage materials: oversize books need oversize shelving, with plenty of supports. Periodicals need perspex covers for current issues and firm plastic storage boxes for back issues. Special storage and display facilities are necessary for audiovisual and non-book stock. A glance through any of the library suppliers' catalogues will reveal a wide range of ingenious solutions to the problems of storing and displaying the increasingly wide range of materials found in library and information units.

The care and repair of stock other than by rebinding or professional conservation procedures is largely a matter of common sense. It is probably true to say that repairing damaged books has become a less significant part of the library assistant's job since the advent of cheap paperback editions – it is often cheaper to replace than repair or indeed send for binding.

In general terms, stock needs to be appropriately shelved and stored:

- all shelves should be kept clean
- temperature and humidity should be maintained at appropriate levels
- direct sunlight should be avoided for paper-based stock – it causes the acid in modern papers to break down, giving a yellowing effect
- the normal library rules concerning the eating of food in the library should be observed – food debris can encourage pests, including really unpleasant ones such as cockroaches and rats!

Good housekeeping procedures are essential, therefore, to the appearance and condition of library stock.

The weeding process

These procedures should include regular and systematic 'weeding' of stock to ensure that everything requiring attention is removed from the shelves and dealt with appropriately. The weeding process plays a vital part in ensuring that not only the physical attractiveness of the stock is maintained, but also its general appropriateness.

Out-of-date material, particularly in scientific and technical subject areas, should not remain on the shelves if the information it contains has become misleading or valueless. But while it is not generally a good idea to keep a book if a revised edition has appeared, in some subject areas outdated material may have a significant historical value and should be retained.

If a date-label check reveals that an item has not been borrowed for some considerable time, this may be another reason to remove it from the shelves, but we must remember that many library professionals believe that there are considerations other than that of maintaining a stock that matches the needs of the user group, in that libraries have a duty to retain the seminal texts of our culture even if they do not appear to be being borrowed. Other factors to consider are changing views on political correctness: some items may need to be discarded on the grounds that they have come to be seen as sexist, racist or inappropriately propagandist. We must also be aware of the need to maintain a balanced stock that accurately reflects the needs of a changing clientèle.

Those items that are removed will be either repaired, rebound, placed on reserve stacks, offered to another library, sold to the public or disposed of by pulping or recycling. The decisions here would normally be taken by professional library staff.

Repair

Library assistants usually become very proficient in appropriate repair techniques of book and non-book materials. It is worth noting that Sellotape should never be used in book repairs, as it becomes brittle and discolours. There are on the market a number of library-specific products such as ghost tape and paper adhesive that can safely be used on tears, loose pages and torn jackets. Marks on pages can often be removed by a soft eraser or a proprietary fluid. There are also a number of folk remedies passed on from the more mature colleague! These include the use of white bread to remove stains from paper, and the ironing of grease marks through blotting paper. However, if the material concerned is at all valuable, it is clear that it is better to seek the specialist expertise normally available from commercial binderies.

Binding and rebinding

The procedures involved in binding and rebinding used to play a very significant part in the work of paraprofessional library staff but, as has been said, the proportion of bookstock going for rebinding has dramatically decreased since the success of paperback publishing, and over the last 30 years many commercial library binders have either ceased to trade or had to diversify into conservation and other specialist services such as the de-acidification of paper and the encapsulation of valuable manuscript material. The effect of this change on the appearance of library stock has been largely beneficial: old-fashioned rebinding styles, particularly for fiction, were often unattractive.

Binding and rebinding are expensive, and there are strict criteria that should be applied to both the rebinding of books and the binding of periodicals and journals. As far as bookstock is concerned, we have to consider what use will be made of material if rebound – the unattractiveness of some second bindings and the preferability of paperback editions have already been noted. Age and present condition are also important – obviously, a book must be complete, and, if it has been rebound before, a further rebind may be impossible owing to trimmed margins. If the book is about to be superseded by a new edition clearly it should not be rebound.

Periodicals and journals form a vital area of stock, particularly in academic and special libraries, where they often contain the most up-to-date material in many subject areas and where it is essential that backfiles are available for research purposes. Nevertheless, a number of considerations must be taken into account before deciding on the binding of back numbers of periodicals. It is very costly and has disadvantages such as the amount of time for which the items are unavailable to users while being bound, and the amount of space taken up by bound volumes. When binding is being considered, we must also check availability on CD-ROM, microform and online. There is also the possibility that neighbouring libraries or information units might keep bound backfiles already, and would allow access. We also need to consider amount of usage – it might be cheaper and more effective to use the British Library to obtain photocopies if the demand is slight – and value (is the periodical concerned of lasting value, for example *National Geographic*, or of ephemeral value, for example *Melody Maker*)? We need a complete run of periodicals, plus appropriate indexes and enough storage to keep the bound volumes.

Although the binding of periodicals is costly, and despite the disadvantages outlined here, it is worth mentioning that lengthy and complete backfiles of bound periodicals can be immensely valuable. The art college library that decided to bind *Vogue* from its first issue in 1916 now possesses a very important archive.

Procedures for dealing with both the binding of periodicals and journals and the rebinding of books are straightforward. Most binding firms call at regular intervals to collect and return materials. Once the material has been selected for binding according to the criteria outlined above, binding lists are compiled – one copy with the material, one retained by the organization – together with specific and detailed instructions to the binder including, for example, type and colour of covering material and type and position of lettering. Uniformity is particularly important when dealing with periodicals, to ensure all backfiles of a title match. It is very important to note on the library catalogue when an item is at binding.

When the consignment of binding is returned it is checked against the binding list and for correct adherence to instructions: the catalogue is adjusted and the items are returned to stock.

Rebindings are a great deal more attractive than they used to be. Dustjackets may be incorporated to give a much brighter appearance. Paperbacks can be specially strengthened without spoiling their appearance, and publications whose rather fragile 'perfect' binding style (in perfect binding the sections of the book are glued rather than sewn) make them unsuitable for heavy library use may be rebound using the original covers before being added to stock.

Bibliography of key reference sources

(reproduced from Tim Buckley Owen's *Success at the Enquiry Desk: successful enquiry answering every time*, 4th edn, Facet Publishing, 2003, with thanks).

Abstracts in New Technologies and Engineering
    Subject index (with brief abstracts from 1993) to articles in UK and
    US science and technology journals. Available in print and online.
    Companion sources: *British Humanities Index, Applied Social
    Sciences Index and Abstracts, Sociological Abstracts*.
    Comparable sources: *Applied Science & Technology Index and
    Abstracts/full text, General Science Abstracts/full text*.
    CSA, 3rd Floor, Farrington House, Wood Street, East Grinstead, West
    Sussex RH19 1UZ. Tel: 01342 310480. Fax: 01342 310487.
    E-mail: sales@csa.com.
    Web: www.csa.com.
Annual Abstract of Statistics
    Comprehensive collection of statistics on all subjects, usually

abstracted from more detailed government statistical publications. Also available online at www.statistics.gov.uk.

Companion sources: *Regional Trends, Social Trends*.

Complementary sources: *Eurostat Yearbook, United Nations Statistical Yearbook*.

Office for National Statistics. Available through TSO, PO Box 29, St Crispin's, Duke Street, Norwich NR3 1GN. Tel: 0870 600 5522. Fax: 0870 600 5533. E-mail: customer.services@tso.co.uk. Web: www.tso.co.uk.

Annual Register

Provides details of the year's events on a country-by-country basis, plus a political, social and economic overview of each country.

Comparable sources: *Europa World Year Book* (much bigger), *Statesman's Yearbook*.

Keesing's Worldwide, 28a Hills Road, Cambridge CB2 1LA. Tel: 01223 508050. Fax: 01223 508049. E-mail: info@keesings.com. Web: www.keesings.com.

Applied Science & Technology Index and Abstracts/full text

Subject index, with abstracts and latterly full text, to articles in English language science and technology journals published worldwide. Available in print, on CD-ROM and online.

Companion sources: *General Science Abstracts/full text, Humanities Index/Abstracts/full text, Social Sciences Index/Abstracts/full text, Wilson OmniFile Full Text Mega Edition*.

Comparable source: *Abstracts in New Technologies and Engineering*.

H W Wilson Co, 950 University Avenue, Bronx, New York 10452. Tel: 00 1 718 588 8400. Fax: 00 1 718 590 1617. E-mail: custserv@hwwilson.com.

UK & European agent: Thompson Henry Ltd, London Road, Sunningdale, Berks SL5 0EP. Tel: 01344 624615. Fax: 01344 626120. E-mail: thl@thompsonhenry.co.uk. Web: www.hwwilson.com.

Applied Social Sciences Index and Abstracts

Subject index, with abstracts, to articles mostly in United Kingdom social science journals. Available in print and online.

Companion sources: *Abstracts in New Technologies and Engineering, British Humanities Index, Sociological Abstracts*.

Comparable source: *Social Sciences Index/Abstracts/full text*.

CSA, 3rd Floor, Farrington House, Wood Street, East Grinstead, West Sussex RH19 1UZ. Tel: 01342 310480. Fax: 01342 310487.

E-mail: sales@csa.com.

Web: www.csa.com.

Aslib Directory of Information Sources in the United Kingdom

Gives details of services available from special libraries and information units, including terms and conditions for access.

Aslib Books & Directories, Aslib/Europa, 11 New Fetter Lane, London EC4P 4EE. Tel: 020 7822 4341. Fax: 020 7822 4329. E-mail: info.europa@tandf.co.uk.

Web: www.europapublications.co.uk.

BBC News Online

Comprehensive general news service updated throughout the day with a fully searchable archive.

Comparable service: *Keesing's Record of World Events*.

Web: http://news.bbc.co.uk.

Benn's Media

Gives full publication details of newspapers and journals by subject.

Competitor: *Willing's Press Guide*.

Comparable source: *Ulrich's Periodicals Directory*.

Annual. 3 vols: United Kingdom, Europe, World.

CMP Information Ltd, Riverbank House, Angel Lane, Tonbridge, Kent TN9 1SE. Tel: 01732 362666. Fax: 01732 367301. E-mail: enquiries@cmpinformation.com.

Web: www.cmpdata.com.

British Humanities Index

Subject index (with abstracts from 1991) to articles in British and other English language humanities journals. Available in print and online.

Companion sources: *Abstracts in New Technologies and Engineering, Applied Social Sciences Index and Abstracts, Sociological Abstracts*.

Comparable source: *Humanities Index/Abstracts/full text*.

CSA, 3rd Floor, Farrington House, Wood Street, East Grinstead, West Sussex RH19 1UZ. Tel: 01342 310480. Fax: 01342 310487.

E-mail: sales@csa.com.

Web: www.csa.com.

British Library – inside web

Subscription-based online service that allows you to search for thousands of journal articles and conference papers by title and order them online.

Comparable services: Emerald, Ingenta, *Wilson OmniFile Full Text Mega Edition*.

Web: www.bl.uk/services/current/inside.html.

British Library Integrated Catalogue
  Includes entries for all the items available from the British Library,
  either for reference, loan or supply as photocopies. Also provides links
  to other leading UK and overseas library catalogues.
  Comparable services: *British National Bibliography*, *Global Books in
  Print*, Whitaker LibWeb.
  Web: http://catalogue.bl.uk/.
British National Bibliography
  Gives details of all books and pamphlets placed on legal deposit in the
  British Library, classified by subject. Available in print and on CD-
  ROM.
  Comparable services: British Library public catalogue, *Global Books in
  Print*, Whitaker LibWeb.
  British Library, National Bibliographic Service, Boston Spa,
  Wetherby, West Yorkshire LS23 7BQ. Tel: 01937 546585. Fax: 01937
  546586. E-mail: nbs-info@bl.uk.
  Web: www.bl.uk.
Centres, Bureaux & Research Institutes
  Gives details of centres of expertise in a wide range of fields.
  Companion sources: *Councils, Committees & Boards, Current British
  Directories, Directory of British Associations & Associations in
  Ireland, Directory of European Industrial & Trade Associations,
  Directory of European Professional & Learned Societies, Pan-
  European Associations*.
  CBD Research Ltd, 15 Wickham Road, Beckenham, Kent BR3 2JS. Tel:
  020 8650 7745. Fax: 020 8650 0768. E-mail: cbd@cbdresearch.com.
  Web: www.cbdresearch.com.
Councils, Committees & Boards
  Gives details of official and public bodies and quangos in the United
  Kingdom.
Current British Directories
  Describes contents of directories and reference works published in the
  UK.
  Comparable source: *Ulrich's Periodicals Directory*.
  Companion sources to both: *Centres, Bureaux & Research Institutes,
  Directory of British Associations & Associations in Ireland, Directory
  of European Industrial & Trade Associations, Directory of European
  Professional & Learned Societies, Pan-European Associations*.
  CBD Research Ltd, 15 Wickham Road, Beckenham, Kent BR3 2JS. Tel:
  020 8650 7745. Fax: 020 8650 0768. E-mail: bd@cbdresearch.com.

Web: www.cbdresearch.com.
Dialog
Dialog DataStar
Dialog Profound
  Multipurpose online information services permitting sophisticated
  searching of thousands of sources with global coverage on all subjects.
  Comparable services: Factiva, LexisNexis.
  Web: www.dialog.com.
Directory of British Associations & Associations in Ireland
Directory of European Industrial & Trade Associations
Directory of European Professional & Learned Societies
  Uniform series giving details of associations, societies and other
  organizations throughout the UK and Europe respectively.
  Companion sources: *Centres, Bureaux & Research Institutes, Councils,
  Committees & Boards, Current British Directories, Pan-European
  Associations.*
  Comparable sources: *Encyclopaedia of Associations: International
  Organizations, Europa Directory of International Organizations, World
  Directory of Trade and Business Associations, Yearbook of International
  Organizations.*
  CBD Research Ltd, 15 Wickham Road, Beckenham, Kent BR3 2JS. Tel:
  020 8650 7745. Fax: 020 8650 0768. E-mail: cbd@cbdresearch.com.
  Web: www.cbdresearch.com.
Emerald
  Provides searchable abstracts and full text of management, technology
  and library & information journal articles.
  Comparable services British Library – Inside web, Ingenta, *Wilson
  OmniFile Full Text Mega Edition.*
  Web: www.emeraldinsight.com.
Encyclopaedia of Associations: International Organizations
  Gives details of professional and trade associations, societies and
  institutions in the United States and internationally.
  Competitors: *Europa Directory of International Organizations,
  Yearbook of International Organizations.*
  Comparable sources: *Pan-European Associations, World Directory of
  Trade & Business Associations.*
  Thomson Learning (EMEA), High Holborn House, 50–51 Bedford
  Row, London WC1R 4LR. Tel: 020 7607 2500. Fax: 020 7067 2600.
  E-mail: galeord@gale.com.
  Web: www.gale.com.

Europa Directory of International Organisations
　Gives details of international and world regional organizations.
　Competitors: *Encyclopaedia of Associations: International*
　Organizations, Yearbook of International Organizations
　Comparable sources: *Pan-European Associations, World Directory of*
　Trade and Business Associations.
Europa World Yearbook
　Describes the political, social and economic life of each country of the
　world, with details of main institutions.
　Comparable sources (but much shorter): *Annual Register, Statesman's*
　Yearbook.
　Complementary source: *UK . . . the Official Yearbook of the United*
　Kingdom of Great Britain and Northern Ireland.
　Companion source to both: *World of Learning.*
　Europa Publications, 11 New Fetter Lane, London EC4P 4EE. Tel:
　020 7822 4300. Fax: 020 7822 4329. E-mail: info.europa@tandf.co.uk.
　Web: www.europapublications.co.uk.
Eurostat Yearbook
　Comprehensive collection of statistics on all subjects, comparing
　European Union member states and usually abstracted from more
　detailed Eurostat publications.
　Complementary sources: *Annual Abstract of Statistics, United Nations*
　Statistical Yearbook.
　Office for National Statistics. Available through TSO (for Eurostat),
　PO Box 29, St Crispin's, Duke Street, Norwich NR3 1GN. Tel: 0870 600
　5522. Fax: 0870 600 5533. E-mail: customer.services@tso.co.uk.
　(Equivalent agents operate in other European Union member states as
　well; see Eurostat website for details.)
　Web: www.tso.co.uk.
　Eurostat web: http://europa.eu.int/comm/eurostat.
Factiva
　Online information service provided by Reuters (UK) and Dow Jones
　(US) permitting sophisticated searching of business information
　sources of all kinds.
　Comparable services: DataStar, Dialog, LexisNexis.
　Web: www.factiva.com.
General Science Abstracts/full text
　Subject index, with abstracts and some full text, to articles in English
　language science journals published worldwide. Available in print, on
　CD-ROM and online.

Companion sources: *Applied Science & Technology Index and Abstracts/full text, Humanities Index/Abstracts/full text, Social Sciences Index/Abstracts/full text, Wilson OmniFile Full Text Mega Edition.*
Comparable source: *Abstracts in New Technologies and Engineering.*
H W Wilson Co, 950 University Avenue, Bronx, New York 10452.
Tel: 00 1 718 588 8400. Fax: 00 1 718 590 1617. E-mail: custserv@hwwilson.com.
UK & European agent: Thompson Henry Ltd, London Road, Sunningdale, Berks SL5 0EP. Tel: 01344 624615. Fax: 01344 626120.
E-mail: thl@thompsonhenry.co.uk.
Web: www.hwwilson.com.

Global Books in Print
Gives bibliographic details of currently available English language books worldwide. Available on CD-ROM and online as www.globalbooksinprint.com.
Comparable services: British Library public catalogue, *British National Bibliography*, Whitaker LibWeb.
Bowker, Windsor Court, East Grinstead House, East Grinstead, West Sussex RH19 1XA. Tel: 01342 336179. Fax: 01342 336198. E-mail: customer.services@bowker.co.uk.
Web: www.bowker.co.uk.

A Guide to Finding Quality Information on the Internet: selection and evaluation strategies
Suggests strategies for locating, selecting and evaluating the quality information on the net. By Alison Cooke.
Companion sources: *Know it All, Find it Fast: an A-Z source guide for the enquiry desk, The Library and Information Professional's Internet Companion, Practical Copyright, The Public Librarian's Guide to the Internet, The New Walford Guide to Reference Resources* .
Facet Publishing, 7 Ridgmount Street, London WC1E 7AE.
Tel: 020 7255 0594. Fax: 020 7255 0591. E-mail: info@facetpublishing.co.uk. Web: www.facetpublishing.co.uk.

Hollis UK Press & Public Relations Annual
Hollis Europe: the Directory of European Public Relations & PR Networks
Companion volumes giving details of public relations departments and press offices of a very large number of organizations. Also available online.
Hollis Directories Ltd, Harlequin House, 7 High Street, Teddington, Middlesex TW11 8EL. Tel: 020 8977 7711. Fax: 020 8977 1133. E-mail: orders@hollis-pr.co.uk.

Web: www.hollis-pr.com.
Humanities Index/Abstracts/full text
Subject index, latterly with abstracts and full text, to articles in English language humanities journals published worldwide. Available in print, on CD-ROM and online.
Companion sources: *Applied Science & Technology Index and Abstracts/full text, General Science Abstracts/full text, Social Sciences Index/Abstracts/full text, Wilson OmniFile Full Text Mega Edition.*
Comparable source: *British Humanities Index.*
H W Wilson Co, 950 University Avenue, Bronx, New York 10452. Tel: 00 1 718 588 8400. Fax: 00 1 718 590 1617. E-mail: custserv@hwwilson.com.
UK & European agent: Thompson Henry Ltd, London Road, Sunningdale, Berks SL5 0EP. Tel: 01344 624615. Fax: 01344 626120. E-mail: thl@thompsonhenry.co.uk.
Web: www.hwwilson.com.
Ingenta
Provides full text of articles from a large number of academic and professional journals.
Comparable services: British Library – inside web, Emerald, Wilson omnifile full text mega edition.
Web: www.ingenta.com.
Keesing's Record of World Events
Provides summaries of news from around the world, with regularly updated subject indexes. Available in print, on CD-ROM and online.
Comparable service: BBC News online.
Keesing's Worldwide, 28a Hills Road, Cambridge CB2 1LA. Tel: 01223 508050. Fax: 01223 508049. E-mail: info@keesings.com.
Web: www.keesings.com.
Know it All, Find it Fast: an A-Z source guide for the enquiry desk
Arranged by subject, suggests a wide range of sources, both printed and electronic, that will help answer some of the commonest enquiries. By Bob Duckett, Peter Walker and Christinea Donnelly.
Companion sources: *A Guide to Finding Quality Information on the Internet: selection and evaluation strategies, Know it All, Find it Fast: an A-Z source guide for the enquiry desk, The Library and Information Professional's Internet Companion, The New Walford Guide to Reference Resources, Practical Copyright.*
Facet Publishing, 7 Ridgmount Street, London WC1E 7AE. Tel: 020 7255 0594. Fax: 020 7255 0591. E-mail: info@facetpublishing.co.uk.

Web: www.facetpublishing.co.uk.

LexisNexis
Multipurpose online information service permitting sophisticated
searching of newspaper and journal articles and legal information
sources; still significant US focus but other coverage improving.
Comparable services DataStar, Dialog and Factiva.
Web: www.lexisnexis.com.

The Library and Information Professional's Internet Companion
Provides comprehensive guidance on how to use the full range of
internet-based services and facilities. By Alan Poulter, Debra Hiom
and David McMenemy.
Companion sources: *A Guide to Finding Quality Information on the
Internet: selection and evaluation strategies, Know it All, Find it Fast:
an A-Z source guide for the enquiry desk, The Public Librarian's
Guide to the Internet, Practical Copyright, The New Walford Guide to
Reference Resources.*
Facet Publishing, 7 Ridgmount Street, London WC1E 7AE. Tel: 020
7255 0594. Fax: 020 7255 0591. E-mail: info@facetpublishing.co.uk.
Web: www.facetpublishing.co.uk.

National Statistics
Provides large number of UK statistics online, plus guidance on the
full range of official statistics available elsewhere as well.
Comparable service: United Nations Statistics Division.
Web: www.statistics.gov.uk.

The New Walford Guide to Reference Resources
Describes mostly English-language reference sources on all subjects,
including websites, organizations, sourcebooks, directories and
yearbooks, journals, statistics and selected textbooks. 3 vols: Science
and technology, and Medicine; The Social Sciences; Arts, Humanities
and General Reference.
Companion sources: *A Guide to Finding Quality Information on the
Internet: selection and evaluation strategies, Know it All, Find it Fast:
an A-Z source guide for the enquiry desk, The Public Librarian's
Guide to the Internet, The New Walford Guide to Reference Resources,
Practical Copyright.* Facet Publishing, 7 Ridgmount Street, London
WC1E 7AE. Tel: 020 7255 0594. Fax: 020 7255 0591. E-mail:
info@facetpublishing.co.uk. Web: www.facetpublishing.co.uk.

Pan-European Associations
Gives details of Europe-wide professional and trade associations,
societies and institutions.

Companion sources: *Centres, Bureaux & Research Institutes, Councils, Committees & Boards, Current British Directories, Directory of British Associations, Directory of European Industrial & Trade Associations, Directory of European Professional & Learned Societies.*
Comparable sources: *Encyclopaedia of Associations: International Organizations, World Directory of Trade and Business Associations, Yearbook of International Organizations.*
CBD Research Ltd, 15 Wickham Road, Beckenham, Kent BR3 2JS. Tel: 020 8650 7745. Fax: 020 8650 0768. E-mail: cbd@cbdresearch.com. Web: www.cbdresearch.com.

Practical Copyright for Information Professionals: the CILIP handbook. By Sandy Norman
A guide to copyright law as it applies to various kinds of library.
Companion sources: *A Guide to Finding Quality Information on the Internet: selection and evaluation strategies, Know it All, Find it Fast: an A-Z source guide for the enquiry desk, The Library and Information Professional's Internet Companion, The Public librarian's Guide to the Internet, The New Walford Guide to Reference Resources.*
Facet Publishing, 7 Ridgmount Street, London WC1E 7AE. Tel: 020 7255 0594. Fax: 020 7255 0591. E-mail: info@facetpublishing.co.uk. Web: www.facetpublishing.co.uk.

The Public Librarian's Guide to the Internet
Covers the basics of the internet and includes advice on the best websites on specific subjects. Useful for far more than just public librarians! By Sally Criddle, Alison McNab, Sarah Ormes, Ian Winship.
Companion sources: *A Guide to Finding Quality Information on the Internet: selection and evaluation strategies, Know it All, Find it Fast: an A-Z source guide for the enquiry desk, The Library and Information Professional's Internet Companion, Practical Copyright, The New Walford Guide to Reference Resources.*
Facet Publishing, 7 Ridgmount Street, London WC1E 7AE. Tel: 020 7255 0594. Fax: 020 7255 0591. E-mail: info@facetpublishing.co.uk. Web: www.facetpublishing.co.uk.

Regional Trends
Comprehensive collection of statistics on all subjects, comparing each of the United Kingdom standard regions. Also available online at www.statistics.gov.uk.
Companion sources: *Annual Abstract of Statistics, Social Trends.*
Office for National Statistics. Available through TSO, PO Box 29, St Crispin's, Duke Street, Norwich NR3 1GN. Tel: 0870 600 5522. Fax:

0870 600 5533. E-mail: customer.services@tso.co.uk.
Web: www.tso.co.uk.

Social Sciences Index/Abstracts/full text
Subject index, latterly with abstracts and full text, to articles in English language social science journals published worldwide. Available in print, on CD-ROM and online.
Companion sources: *Applied Science & Technology Index and Abstracts/full text, General Science Abstracts, Humanities Index/Abstracts/full text, Wilson OmniFile Full Text Mega Edition.*
Comparable sources: *Applied Social Sciences Index and Abstracts, Sociological Abstracts.*
H W Wilson Co, 950 University Avenue, Bronx, New York 10452. Tel: 00 1 718 588 8400. Fax: 00 1 718 590 1617. E-mail: custserv@hwwilson.com.
UK & European agent: Thompson Henry Ltd, London Road, Sunningdale, Berks SL5 0EP. Tel: 01344 624615. Fax: 01344 626120. E-mail: thl@thompsonhenry.co.uk.
Web: www.hwwilson.com.

Social Trends
Selection of statistics on a wide range of British social issues, taken from more detailed government statistical publications. Also available online at www.statistics.gov.uk.
Companion sources: *Annual Abstract of Statistics, Regional Trends.*
Complementary source: *World Marketing Data and Statistics.*
Office for National Statistics. Available through TSO, PO Box 29, St Crispin's, Duke Street, Norwich NR3 1GN. Tel: 0870 600 5522. Fax: 0870 600 5533. E-mail: customer.services@tso.co.uk.
Web: www.tso.co.uk.

Sociological Abstracts
Subject index, with abstracts, to articles, books, chapters and conference papers internationally on the social and behavioural sciences. Available in print and online.
Companion sources: *Abstracts in New Technologies and Engineering, Applied Social Sciences Index and Abstracts, British Humanities Index.*
Comparable source: *Social Sciences Index/Abstracts/full text.*
CSA, 3rd Floor, Farrington House, Wood Street, East Grinstead, West Sussex RH19 1UZ. Tel: 01342 310480. Fax: 01342 310487.
E-mail: sales@csa.com.
Web: www.csa.com.

Sources of Non-Official UK Statistics
Gives details of non-governmental statistical sources, mostly relating to business and industry. By David Mort.
Complementary source: *World Directory of Non-Official Statistical Sources.*
Gower Publishing Ltd, Gower House, Croft Road, Aldershot, Hants GU11 3HR. Tel: 01252 331551. Fax: 01252 344405. E-mail: info@gowerpub.com.
Web: www.gowerpub.com.

Statesman's Yearbook
Describes the political, social and economic life of each country of the world, with details of main institutions.
Comparable sources: *Annual Register, Europa World Yearbook* (much bigger).
Complementary source: *UK... the Official Yearbook of the United Kingdom of Great Britain and Northern Ireland.*
Palgrave Macmillan Ltd, Houndmills, Basingstoke, Hampshire, RG21 6XS. Tel: Tel: 01256 329242. Fax: 01256 328339. E-mail: bookenquiries@palgrave.com.
Web: www.palgrave.com.

UK . . . the Official Yearbook of the United Kingdom of Great Britain and Northern Ireland
Describes British political, social and economic life and gives details of principal United Kingdom institutions.
Complementary sources: *Europa World Yearbook, Statesman's Yearbook.*
Office for National Statistics. Available through TSO, PO Box 29, St Crispin's, Duke Street, Norwich NR3 1GN. Tel: 0870 600 5522. Fax: 0870 600 5533. E-mail: customer.services@tso.co.uk.
Web: www.tso.co.uk.

Ulrich's Periodicals Directory
Gives details of major journals, directories and yearbooks published worldwide by subject. Also available on disc and online at www.ulrichsweb.com.
Comparable sources: *Benn's Media, Current British Directories, Willing's Press Guide.*
Bowker, Windsor Court, East Grinstead House, East Grinstead, West Sussex RH19 1XA. Tel: 01342 336179. Fax: 01342 336198. E-mail: customer.services@bowker.co.uk.
Web: www.bowker.co.uk.

United Nations Statistics Division
Provides online a range of international comparative statistical data
on a wide variety of topics.
Comparable service: National Statistics.
Web: http://unstats.un.org/ unsd.

United Nations Statistical Yearbook
Comprehensive collection of statistics on all subjects, comparing most
countries of the world. Many statistics also available online from the
United Nations Statistics Division at http://unstats.un.org/unsd.
Complementary sources: *Annual Abstract of Statistics, Eurostat
Yearbook*.
United National Department of Economic & Social Affairs Statistics
Division. TSO, PO Box 29, St Crispin's, Duke Street, Norwich NR3
1GN. Tel: 0870 600 5522. Fax: 0870 600 5533. E-mail:
customer.services@tso.co.uk.
Web: www.tso.co.uk.

Whitaker LibWeb
Online service giving details of current and out-of-print UK books,
and US titles as well.
Comparable services: British Library Integrated catalogue, *British
National Bibliography, Global Books in Print*.
Web: www.whitaker.co.uk/libweb1.htm.

Whitaker's Almanack
Comprehensive repository of brief information on all subjects, from a
British point of view; a good starting point for information for which
there is no obvious specialist source.
A&C Black, 37 Soho Square, London W1D 3QZ. Tel: 020 7758 0200.
E-mail: whitakers@acblack.com.
Web: www.acblack.com.

Willing's Press Guide
Gives full publication details of newspapers and journals by subject. 3
vols: UK, Europe & World. Also available online.
Competitor: *Benn's Media*.
Comparable source: *Ulrich's Periodicals Directory*.
Waymaker Ltd, Chess House, 34 Germain Street, Chesham, Bucks
HP5 1SJ. Tel: 0870 7360010. Fax: 01342 335612. E-mail:
willings@waymaker.co.uk.
Web: www.willingspress.com.

Wilson OmniFile Full Text Mega Edition
Includes subject index entries and, where available, abstracts and full

text drawn from the full range of H W Wilson services, including
*General Science Abstracts/full text, Humanities Index/Abstracts/full
text* and *Social Sciences Index/Abstracts/full text*. Available online only.
Comparable services: British Library – inside web, Emerald, Ingenta.
H W Wilson Co, 950 University Avenue, Bronx, New York 10452. Tel:
00 1 718 588 8400. Fax: 00 1 718 590 1617. E-mail:
custserv@hwwilson.com.
UK & European agent: Thompson Henry Ltd, London Road,
Sunningdale, Berks SL5 0EP. Tel: 01344 624615. Fax: 01344 626120.
E-mail: thl@thompsonhenry.co.uk.
Web: www.hwwilson.com.

World Directory of Non-Official Statistical Sources
Gives references to statistics from non-government sources worldwide.
Complementary source: *Sources of Non-Official UK Statistics*.

World Directory of Trade and Business Associations
Gives details of trade and business associations worldwide.
Comparable sources: *Directory of European Industrial & Trade
Associations, Encyclopaedia of Associations: International
Organizations, Europa Directory of International Organizations, Pan-
European Associations, Yearbook of International Organizations*.

World Marketing Data and Statistics
Gives demographic, socio-economic and financial facts and figures for
countries worldwide. Also available online.
Complementary source: *Social Trends*.
Euromonitor plc, 60–61 Britton Street, London EC1M 5NA. Tel: 020
7251 8024. Fax: 020 7608 3149. E-mail: info@euromonitor.com.
Web: www.euromonitor.com.

World of Learning
Gives details of universities, colleges, learned societies, research
institutes and museums worldwide. Also available online at
www.worldoflearning.com.
Companion sources: *Europa Directory of International Organizations,
Europa World Yearbook*.
Europa Publications, 11 New Fetter Lane, London EC4P 4EE. Tel:
020 7822 4300. Fax: 020 7822 4329. E-mail: info.europa@tandf. co.uk.
Web: www.europapublications.co.uk.

Yearbook of International Organizations
Gives contact details and activities of organizations worldwide. Also
available on CD-ROM and online at www.uia.org.
Competitors: *Encyclopaedia of Associations: International*

Organizations, Europa Directory of International Organizations
Comparable sources: *Directory of European Industrial & Trade
Associations, Directory of European Professional & Learned Societies,
Pan-European Associations, World Directory of Trade and Business
Associations.*
Union of International Associations and K G Saur Verlag,
Ortlerstrasse 8; D-81373 München, Germany. Tel: 00 49 089 769020.
Fax: 00 49 089 76902 150. E-mail: info@saur.de. Web: www.saur.de.

References

Anglo-American Cataloguing Rules (1998) Joint Steering Committee for
the Revision of AACR, *Anglo-American Cataloguing Rules*, 2nd edn,
2002 Revision, 2004 Update, London, Facet Publishing on behalf of
CILIP, jointly with American Library Association and Canadian
Library Association.

Owen, T. B. (2003) *Success at the Enquiry Desk: successful enquiry
answering every time*, 4th edn, London, Facet Publishing.

Prytherch, R. J. (1995) *Harrod's Librarians' Glossary*, 8th edn,
Aldershot, Gower.

5 Services to users

We now turn to the range of services offered to users by library and information units.

Customer care and communication skills

A considerable percentage of library and information staff at most levels find themselves dealing directly with their users in a variety of contexts. This is particularly true of paraprofessional staff, who are usually the staff who operate counter services or deal directly with users in other face-to-face situations.

An increasing emphasis on the necessity of a high level of appropriate interpersonal skills has become a feature of the sector in recent years, partly as a result of the business ethics now applied – it is likely that the users of library and information units will be termed clients or customers rather than readers or users – and partly as a result of the influence of American attitudes to customer/provider relationships. Many organizations within the UK library and information sector require their staff to attend customer care courses as part of in-service training, or to undertake Customer Service NVQs. Communication skills also form part of the current City and Guilds 7371 syllabus.

What, then, are the interpersonal skills that library and information staff need to bring to their interaction with their users? It is sometimes difficult for those of us who work in them to realize that libraries do not always seem to be friendly and welcoming places. Surveys all too frequently reveal that users are reluctant to ask for help, partly because they do not want to look foolish and uninformed and partly, for a variety of reasons, because they do not see library staff as approachable. We will be discussing later in this chapter the ways in which library design can help to overcome this image problem, but clearly the most significant way in which the situation can be improved is by setting high standards of interpersonal skills for library and information staff.

Library and information staff need to be polite (but never obsequious on the one hand or patronizing on the other), friendly (but always professional) and always able to behave in a courteous, patient and tactful manner. This behaviour must be able to accommodate the particular requirements of a wide range of users (hearing-impaired, sight-impaired, with learning or mental health difficulties, wheelchair-bound, elderly, with a poor command of English or speech difficulties). This is emphasized by the requirements of the Disability Discrimination Act.

The amount and level of help given in meeting the needs of the user should be precisely that which is required, always bearing in mind any inevitable time constraints and the need to balance the needs of the customer with the needs of the organization. Library and information staff need to give the user their complete attention – with proper but not excessive eye contact – during the interaction. To deal with that interaction, even if it consists only of issuing a book, while simultaneously having a conversation with a colleague is extremely poor in terms of customer care.

There are specific techniques appropriate to the handling of reference and information enquiries which will be discussed later in this chapter. However, clear diction and expression, focused attention, sensitive questioning, an ability to adapt one's approach according to the particular user requirement and an emphasis on keeping the customer informed are important in all interactions. Library and information staff need to be able to deal appropriately with stressful situations, remembering the impropriety of any dispute being conducted in front of other users, the need to defuse problems through a tactful and sensitive approach and the need to observe confidentiality.

The normal guidelines for face-to-face contact may be adapted to telephone contact and to some extent to written, fax or e-mail contact, where clarity, accuracy, correct English and appropriate format are also important.

It is also part of customer care to monitor customer satisfaction – normally done in a library context through user surveys – and to take action to improve problem areas. Most organizations also operate a complaints procedure.

Many organizations operate a dress code intended to give the user the right message concerning the efficiency and professionalism of the staff. Others regard a dress code as an infringement of personal freedom and rely on staff behaviour and approach to deliver the same message.

Although it is clear that the skills we have discussed are both necessary and appropriate – indeed we should welcome this focus as helping to relegate firmly to the past the 'dragon' image of female counter assistants – we should also realize that though clear basic guidelines are necessary, we each bring to our relationships with our users a unique approach that springs from our individuality. No-one would suggest that the current detailed focus on customer-care skills means that we should all react and behave identically. There is also within the sector some unease concerning the appropriateness of customer-care skills designed for business sectors (in the main, retail) to a library and information context, where to some extent a different culture prevails. Should library counter staff, for example, address their users as 'Sir' and 'Madam', or has the deference (even subservience) that lingers on in commercial contexts no place here?

Lending

Historically, libraries were the conservators of material: their lending function, in the sense we use the term today, is comparatively recent and developed with the establishment and growth of the public library movement over the last 150 years. Today, libraries fulfil many aspects of their leisure and educational roles through lending services.

Initially, the lending function of libraries was confined to books, as library stock consisted only of books. In the UK, the Public Libraries Acts have established that the lending of books to people living or working in the catchment area is a free and mandatory service. The development of the lending function and its establishment as, in the public view, the major part of library provision have had, as one would expect, a major impact on the organization, administration and management of public and academic libraries. The development over the last century of subject-based classification schemes, for example, was in part sparked off by the subject-based demand of library borrowers. The development of issue systems, from simple self-service through manual ticket systems such as Browne to the present range of computer charging systems, has been necessitated by the lending function, as has the need to establish guidelines concerning borrower eligibility, number of loans allowed and length of issue period.

The lending function has always had to strike a balance between the educational and the leisure and recreational functions of library services. During the first half of the 20th century, circulating libraries such as those in Boots the Chemist played a large role in serving the recreational needs of readers. With their demise, public libraries have in the main tried to provide their readers with what they want, be it light romance or monographs to support Open University courses, and to balance these demands within financial constraints without in any way making value judgements as to their relative importance. Recent government initiatives have emphasized both aspects. Libraries are clearly seen as vital players in the development of lifelong learning opportunities, and equally as tools for social inclusion (see below).

The modern lending function in both public and academic libraries has come a long way from the rather unsophisticated provision of books only, often in drab bindings and labelled with fierce warnings about infectious diseases, to its present ambitious state. It now embraces a wide variety of non-book material such as videos, compact discs, DVDs and slides – a development which not only widens the range of cultural provision on offer but which also provides a useful opportunity for income generation. Computerized library systems have made it possible to establish various categories of reader with different borrowing entitlements, and various categories of lending stock with differing loan periods. This latter is particularly useful in academic libraries, where it is common practice to have short-loan collections, with loan periods ranging from an hour to a day, in order to meet the borrowing needs of students. The range of loan services currently available is further extended by the interlibrary loan services already discussed.

In short, the lending function of libraries is now impressively comprehensive in terms of both type of material and subject coverage, and in its operation, which can be geared specifically to the needs of individual types of user: the operation of the lending function has been improved immeasurably by the computerization of issue systems.

Reference and research

We have already discussed the stock provided for reference and research purposes in Chapter 4: here we consider the utilization of that stock for the benefit of the user.

Most library and information units operate a reference/research service, ranging from dealing with quick reference queries at a general counter in a small public library, through the provision of separate reference and enquiry desks in larger units, to the detailed and specialist subject-based service, involving complex literature searches, translations and the provision of abstracts, offered by university and special libraries. In all cases, the basic function is the same. To quote the Introduction of a previous edition of Tim Buckley Owen's *Success at the Enquiry Desk* (2003) – a book we would thoroughly recommend as an ideal introduction to working at a reference desk – 'Mediaeval monks in chained libraries wrestled with exactly the same problems as online searchers do today – how to satisfy your enquirer with the right information at the right level, on time. The only difference is that we now have infinitely more flexible tools with which to do the job.' The tools of reference work are not only more flexible but also infinitely more complex and varied with the development of electronic sources such as CD-ROM and the internet.

Successful reference work has been likened to solving the plot of a detective story, and the apparent ease with which reference staff provide obscure information usually impresses the customer! For many library and information staff this is one of the most rewarding and enjoyable elements of their role. Whether in the general reference and enquiry work of public libraries, or in the specialist services offered in information units and academic and special libraries, there is a great deal of job satisfaction in gaining the expertise that offers an informed and professional service.

Even when an enquiry cannot be immediately answered from existing resources, the reference/information assistant should be in the position, to paraphrase a well-known advertisement, of knowing a man who can! In other words, they should be familiar with the use of external sources of information.

In order to ensure that the reference service meets the needs of the customer, it is necessary not just to provide the reference stock, be it specialist or general, printed or electronic, but to ensure that the staff providing this service are able to exploit fully and appropriately the resources available to them, either directly or indirectly.

All the interpersonal skills discussed above come into play in the efficient operation of a reference service. In addition there are specific skills and techniques required. Whatever the nature of the reference query, the reference assistant (using the patience, courtesy, tact and adaptability already discussed) must bring into play the focused listening skills required to clarify the nature of the enquiry. A number of questions may need to be answered at this early stage:

1 Who needs the information? It is surprising, especially in general reference work, how often the person asking at the reference desk is not actually asking on his or her own behalf.
2 At what level is the information required? It is one of the pitfalls of reference work, particularly for the inexperienced member of staff, to misjudge level (to offer, for example, the *Dorling-Kindersley Pocket Book of Butterflies and Moths* instead of a postgraduate monograph on the cabbage white, or indeed the other way around).
3 In what detail is the information needed? It would again be unhelpful to offer a brief encyclopaedia entry on, for example, Impressionism to an enquirer writing a thesis on Monet or, equally, a postgraduate thesis on terrestrial crustaceans to a seven-year-old doing a school project on woodlice! Information overload is as unacceptable as an inadequate response.
4 What precisely does the enquirer want? This again may not be straightforward, as a surprising number of people have a lateral and/or imprecise approach to the information they need and careful and patient questioning may be needed before the true nature of the enquiry emerges. For example, the initial enquiry may be for material on guns while what is really required are newspaper accounts of tragedies such as Hungerford or Dunblane involving the use of firearms. Tim Owen identifies seven types of enquirer who can cause problems in this context – types that reference and enquiry staff will immediately recognize – of whom careful questioning may be needed before we can establish exactly what is wanted. Perhaps the most common of these types are: the generalist, who asks for material on art in general when s/he needs to know precisely which gallery houses Rembrandt's *The Night Watch*; the muddler, who does not know exactly what s/he does want; the obsessively secretive; the know-all; and the casualty of words which either sound very similar or have more than one meaning – for example, whales and Wales, or China as in the country and china as in porcelain. We once spent some time finding information on the philosopher Nietzsche for a bemused enquirer who had actually asked, in an unfamiliar accent, for books on nature!
5 How quickly is the information needed? It would be futile to respond to an enquiry with the offer of an interlibrary loan if the information is required immediately. It is part of appropriate customer care to inform

the enquirer of the progress of the enquiry if it cannot be satisfied straight away.

6 In what form is the information acceptable? It would be useless to provide a microfiche if the enquirer had no access to a microfiche reader.

It is not, however, normally part of our responsibilities to ask for what purpose the information is required except insofar as this information helps us to gauge the detail and level of the information required. This can be difficult in sensitive areas such as child abuse, where the same information may be requested for both perfectly legitimate and less wholesome reasons. Neither should there be any favouritism in our dealings with users – all enquirers should receive the same sympathetic and informed attention whatever their perceived status.

Our initial questioning of the enquirer to establish the precise nature of the enquiry needs to be sensitive, appropriate and non-intrusive. Once we have, to our satisfaction, determined this, an established, efficient, systematic and flexible search strategy should be followed. Most large reference services use enquiry forms to record the name and full details of the enquirer, full details of the enquiry, sources consulted and action taken. It is clearly essential to record in this way for a number of reasons – to prevent duplication of effort, for example, and to record types of query for stock provision purposes.

A search strategy should start with sources available in the organization's own stock (and this would include any specialist subject knowledge possessed by individual members of library staff) and proceed where necessary to outside specialist sources. In fact, part of the expertise of a reference assistant is detailed familiarity with outside sources of information as well as with his or her own reference stock.

Finally, successful fulfilment of reference and information queries is one of the performance indicators of an efficiently functioning service, and certainly one of the aspects of library and information work that most directly affects user satisfaction. While it should be our aim never to send away a dissatisfied customer and to achieve a 100% success rate, in reality we must accept that some information for which we may be asked does not actually exist in the form requested. At Somerset College of Arts and Technology a student was once sent to the reference desk by a lecturer to ask for the immediate supply of statistics concerning the number of people in West Somerset who went on wine-tasting holidays in Burgundy in 1967! Part of reference work, therefore, is, as Tim Owen says, to prepare your enquirer for disappointment if this should on rare occasions prove necessary.

Information

There is clearly an overlap between information giving and reference and research services. In this section we will concentrate on specific information services as distinct from the more general reference and research support offered in most types of library at a range of levels.

Digital information services

A significant development over the past decade has been the emergence of digital reference services. These services first became popular in the academic sector but more recently they have been adapted for use in the public sector and are now increasingly offered as part of the core service.

When public libraries first started supplying digital reference services they took the form mainly of e-mail addresses where enquirers could leave an enquiry and receive a reply by return. This has developed into live online reference services with most libraries using commercially available reference software. This offers opportunities previously unavailable with the traditional reference desk. Librarians using this technology can reach out to enquirers who cannot or do not wish to use the physical library. They can send URLs or take over the screen of the user and direct them through searches and web sites relevant to their enquiry. It offers opportunities for extended hours and appeals particularly to younger users – a traditionally hard-to-reach group – who are growing up in the digital environment.

Librarians, while fundamentally doing what they have always done, must now learn new skills to operate in this virtual transaction. They must learn to work without voice or facial cues from the enquirer and must also develop the skills to multi-task – using the software while answering the enquiry at the same time. They must be skilled in online searching, able to make a swift evaluation of a site and be proficient on the keyboard. There are similarities, however, with traditional services, and just as in a face-to-face service the success of the interaction will depend on cues and proficiency of staff.

An excellent example of a digital reference service is the AnswersNow service offered by Somerset Libraries in partnership with library services in Brisbane Australia, Richland County in South Carolina USA and

Christchurch Libraries in New Zealand. This service, which began in November 2002, uses the different time zones to offer a 24/7 enquiry service throughout the year. Dividing the day into four equal shifts, each authority staffs the 'desk' for six hours each day. The service is accessed via the AnswersNow logo on the webpage of each of the partner authorities, and during a shift the librarian on duty will answer enquiries from any of the partner authorities. Tutor.com, the company that provides the software for the service, also provides professional librarians to pick up any enquiries which come through when the libraries are closed. In this way a genuine 24/7 service is achieved throughout the year. The service is particularly suited to questions of a ready reference nature, with enquirers directed to their home library service for the answers to more in-depth research-type questions.

At the end of 2004 the first phase of a new national digital information service, The People's Network Online Enquiry Service, was launched to library professionals in the UK. Developed by the Museums, Libraries and Archives Council (MLA) and managed by the Co-East development team (one of the sub-regional co-operative groups in the former LASER area), it was launched to the public in late Spring 2005, following a pilot period with participating library authorities.

Tourist information

In Chapter 1 we discussed the provision of tourist information by Tourist Information Centres and we noted that it is not unusual for these to be sited within libraries and operated by the same staff.

Business information

Libraries play a significant role in the provision of business information.

Clearly the library sector has two functions here. First, the commercial sector must be supplied with the information it requires, whether this is at a very local level, with a small public library meeting the information needs of local industry, or in a wider context, with major specialist libraries meeting the complex and extensive information needs of major industrial and commercial centres. It is significant that there is an increasing tendency to regard business information as a commodity and to charge accordingly, making a distinction between the free reference and enquiry service provided for the public and business information which is purchased by the commercial user.

Second, librarians can bring their expertise to help the commercial sector in the efficient and cost-effective management of its own information.

Community information

Libraries, especially public libraries, have a duty to provide community information, and this will be dealt with fully in the next section where we will deal with the community role in general.

Careers information

The other major area in which libraries provide information is that of careers. Careers information services may be found in careers offices, schools, colleges and universities as well as in libraries, and cover careers information, careers planning, loans, grants and sponsorship, employment and training, working and studying abroad, higher and further education, and graduate information. A wide range of information, both local and national, is supplied through printed sources, mainly frequently updated leaflets and reference material, and electronic sources such as the UK higher education courses database ECCTIS. Careers information is a specialist area – it has its own classification scheme, CLCI – and is managed by specialists.

Conclusions

In concluding this outline of the information provision function of libraries and information units we note two things. First, the sources used are increasingly likely to be electronic rather than printed. Second, while public and academic libraries perform an information-providing role among many other roles, in special libraries and information units the provision of information is frequently the major function.

The community role in the UK

Public libraries have always been seen as having a role in the community wider than that of the provision of books, and this emphasis seems currently to be very much on the increase for a number of reasons and in a variety of ways.

Any community role undertaken by local college and school libraries is likely to be decreasing in the face of financial pressures, although there are a number of jointly provided school and community libraries with shared budgets and staffing that operate very successfully in small communities.

How do public libraries fulfil their community role? There has long been a history of involvement with local groups such as playgroups, schools and local societies. This involvement has taken the form of joint activities, the provision of accommodation for meetings and the provision of display facilities. Library staff may be closely involved with local cultural and community activities. Local community information is normally displayed in libraries, and often directories of local information are compiled by and held in libraries. Legal and social security 'surgeries' may be held on a regular basis in libraries, and there is increasing pressure for libraries to involve themselves in this sort of activity.

There is new pressure on libraries in the UK to respond more strongly and specifically to local community needs in the context of a variety of perceived social and economic problems, such as inner city deprivation, inequality of opportunity, truancy and 'latchkey' children, for example. Increasingly, libraries are taking a proactive rather than a reactive role and going out into the community rather than waiting for the community to come to the library. This is evidenced by the increasing popularity of after-school homework clubs and computer clubs, which have been particularly successful and effective in deprived and inner city areas.

Many libraries and library staff are responding in new and radical ways to these challenges, and this is clearly a focus for the future and part of what may be a shift of emphasis in the library role, as libraries try to shake off their undeserved stuffy and middle-class image, and emerge with new priorities to take a vital community role.

These initiatives take several major forms. Even younger children have been targeted by initiatives such as Bookstart, which started in Birmingham distributing free books, library membership cards and early reading tips to new parents in the area and is now being taken up by libraries across the country, involving co-operation between health visitors and librarians, and clearly bringing pleasure and social and educational benefits to both parents and children.

Community initiatives are not limited to conventionally deprived areas such as inner cities. Rural isolation and poverty of opportunity may also be addressed. Shropshire County Library Service has been at the forefront in developing rural community initiatives. Its library network has been utilized to launch Community Information Points, allowing access to a wide range of community information.

Current government thinking emphasizes the role of libraries in achieving social inclusion, and the last few years have seen many significant initiatives undertaken to offer library services to all sections of the community. In May 2004's *Library and Information Update* there is an excellent article by Helen Carpenter (Carpenter, 2004) detailing the efforts of five London boroughs (Brent, Camden, Enfield, Merton and Newham) to improve services to refugees and asylum seekers through their Welcome to Your Library scheme. In *Library and Information Update* in January 2004 Tricia Kings (Kings, 2004) describes how public libraries can work with prisoners to involve them in their children's reading. The Big Book Share has been shown to strengthen both family bonds and prisoners' own self-esteem, making it more likely that they will settle back into the community after release.

There has also been a focus on services to the gypsy and traveller communities. CILIP's Libraries Change Lives Award for 2004 went to Essex for its Mobile Library Travellers Project. An article in *Library and Information Update* in October 2004 describes in detail this successful scheme (Baker, 2004). There is more prejudice expressed against gypsies and travellers than against any other minority group, with refugees and asylum seekers a close second, as John Pateman's recent article in *Update* shows (Pateman, 2004). Pateman argues strongly for the mainstreaming of provision for all socially excluded groups.

Library building and design

Current library building and design in the UK are clearly affected by two issues we have already discussed: the funding crisis and the changing nature of libraries themselves.

The funding crisis may be addressed to a small degree by changes in National Lottery award criteria introduced by the Labour government. Bidding for grants is now very much a feature, and when successful (as recently in Sevenoaks, Kent) can have great results. However, it is not difficult to find public library buildings which have become extremely shabby and run down.

As far as changes in the purpose and function of libraries are concerned, it is vital that current library design should be sophisticated, flexible and sensitive to the library's developing and rapidly changing role. To this end, it is vital that librarians act as consultants to the architects involved. Only then will proper provision for new technologies, and new community initiatives such as those already discussed, be catered for alongside the traditional print-based provision.

Library building and design will also be influenced by the changing emphases on user friendliness and customer care. Old-style libraries, with their rigorous stress on regulations such as the much-derided silence rule, their often unwelcoming – even offputting – atmosphere and their separation of staff and customer, are now clearly seen as inappropriate. What is needed now is a more welcoming approach with an emphasis on accessibility and informality, an approach inclusive of the whole community served: design and buildings must reflect this, whether they be in the public or academic sector. It is becoming increasingly common to find libraries alongside supermarkets, or in shopping malls, such as in Cambridge. Health and safety issues are increasingly important, as are the legal requirements for access for the disabled.

The future seems likely to see increasing use of Private Finance Initiatives, which use private money to erect public buildings – for example, the splendid new library at Brighton was funded in this way.

References

Baker, N. (2004) Breaking the Cycle of Poor Literacy, *Library and Information Update*, **3** (10), October, 38–9.

Carpenter, H. (2004) Welcome to Your Library, *Library and Information Update*, **3** (5), May, 40–1.

Kings, T. (2004) Inside Out: the Big Book Share, *Library and Information Update*, **3** (1), January, 24–6.

Owen, T. B. (2003) *Success at the Enquiry Desk: successful enquiry answering every time*, 4th edn, London, Facet Publishing.

Pateman, J. (2004) Tackling Exclusion: gypsies and travellers, *Library and Information Update*, **3** (3), March, 42–3.

6 Information technology in the library

Alan Hornsey

The pace of change in the world of IT has not let up since the last (2001) edition of this book: new trends have emerged while old ones have gathered strength or faded. Increases in the processing speed and power of computers have continued, with 64-bit processors now on sale, and huge amounts of digital storage available relatively cheaply; the concept of the 'thin client' (of which more later) also seems to be making something of a comeback; wireless networks (wifi) have burgeoned; and broadband connectivity to the internet is becoming the norm in institutional settings. Software has developed at a similar rate: new versions of operating systems from both Microsoft and Apple are either here now or soon will be, but increasingly programs are available with a web browser interface and so are operating-system agnostic. The other big story here is the increasing use of free and open source software (FOSS), such as the Linux operating system and Firefox web browser.

The rate of change remains too rapid for most libraries to keep abreast of the cutting edge of technology, because of the expense if nothing else, and older solutions will probably be found co-existing with newer. For example, CD-ROMs have retained their usefulness despite the popularity of DVDs, and wireless connectivity may well complement rather than completely replace wired network infrastructures.

Predictions of the demise of the traditional bricks and mortar library as a distinct physical repository, to be replaced by the 'virtual library' existing only in cyberspace, seem to have been premature: the concept of the 'digital library' has been developing steadily, but it is more likely to be produced by and accessed from a physical library than to replace it.

Libraries today are usually 'dual-format' – depositories for printed information and access points to the world of electronic resources, places where optical media can be borrowed as well as used and where computer hardware is available to produce new information.

In the UK the success of the People's Network has made this as true of the high street library as of special or academic or national institutions. This initiative has also led to an increase in IT training for library staff and computer literacy is no longer an optional extra: those with no IT qualifications or experience before employment will find IT familiarization an integral part of their induction and continuing development.

As always, new positive developments in IT have been accompanied by new problems and an increase in some old ones: viruses and spam continue to plague the world of e-mail, while the new practice of 'phishing' and the possibility of identity theft has emerged to trouble the web. As a result an emphasis on security has now become all-pervading in IT, with firewalls and anti-malware programs an essential part of a computer or network installation.

The aim of this chapter is to introduce those with little or no IT experience to the basic terms and concepts associated with the field, and, for those with some experience, to show the applications of IT to libraries and information units. Incidentally, you may be familiar with the abbreviations ICT (information and communication technology) and, particularly in an academic context, ILT (information and learning technology). I shall continue here to use the traditional IT, but it should be understood to embrace both ICT and ILT.

Basic terms and concepts

There are many different types of hardware and software in use in the library IT environment, and until recently the trend was towards standardization of both the software and hardware in the form of the 'Wintel' platform. This consisted of a PC with a microprocessor (chip) made by Intel and one of the Windows operating systems made by Microsoft. Computers capable of running the Windows OS (operating system) used to be called IBM-compatible or IBM PCs. Today they're made by many different manufacturers, competition which has led to their low price, and are usually just called PCs, even though there's a risk of confusion with the general concept of a personal computer, which includes other types of hardware platform such as that of the PowerPC used by

Apple. AMD now also make chips for the PC in competition with Intel: they're usually less expensive and often more powerful, and run Windows and other OSs just as well.

The operating system is the most fundamental program (or suite of programs) on a computer; all other programs operate 'on top' of the OS. There's no need to start this program yourself – it's what starts up when you switch the machine on and takes you to a logon screen or straight to a graphical desktop, which itself is part of the OS. It provides the software environment within which all other programs operate, allowing them to run simultaneously (multi-tasking), and providing access to the hardware, peripherals and disk and file management facilities.

Windows became the de facto standard for the PC operating system and is still the norm in libraries in the UK, but dissatisfaction with its security vulnerabilities, complex licensing arrangements, cost and fear of being 'locked in' to a monopolistic vendor, have led to the development of alternatives. The Apple Macintosh (called 'Apple' or 'Mac') has long been popular, especially among the graphic design community, and Apple is now trying to make inroads into the general computer and server markets; ease of use is its big selling-point, the disadvantage being that the OS cannot be run on a cheap commodity PC, but only on Apple's own relatively expensive hardware. It has recently been announced that Apple is to move over to Intel chips from the IBM PowerPC microprocessor; this should lower prices but the OS will probably still only be available for Apple-manufactured PCs.

The real growth is in the use of the open source Linux OS: this has been developed by a global community of companies and individuals and is available for little or no charge. In addition its licensing terms allow you to install it on as many PCs as you like and to pass it on to others as you wish. It has been 'ported' to a myriad of hardware devices, from mainframes and supercomputers to mobile phones and embedded devices (chips found in electronic hardware). It is used by many organizations across the world, including NASA, IBM and Novell, and is just as accessible to home computer users. Despite its earlier reputation for being difficult to install and use, it has become extremely user-friendly, with its GUIs (graphical user interfaces) rivalling those of Microsoft or Apple (in fact with Linux you have a choice of several GUIs). The chances are that its acceptance will only continue to grow and that it is just a matter of time before it is seen in most libraries; at the moment it is held back by lack of familiarity, its lack of the same programs that are available for Windows and the fact that it is difficult to buy a PC with anything other than some version of Windows pre-installed.

Hardware

Most computers to be encountered in libraries today will be in the form of PCs based around a microprocessor (hence microcomputer or just micro); they will have a colour monitor, keyboard and mouse, all plugged into a box on which the monitor sits or a tower design standing upright next to the monitor or on the floor. This box contains disk drives (hard drives, floppy drives, CD-ROM or DVD drives), plug-in cards (such as modems and network cards) which expand their capabilities and, most importantly, the motherboard with its array of memory chips (RAM or random access memory, where the programs run) and the central processing unit (CPU). The box itself is sometimes loosely referred to as the CPU, but this really refers to the micro, which does all the calculating and integrates all the separate components and operations of the PC. Each OS is designed to run on a particular make of CPU.

In the distant past users had to type commands into a command-line interface (CLI – like DOS for those of you who remember Microsoft's pre-Windows systems); these are still available for expert users, but these days you're almost certain to be using a GUI instead (graphical user interface – also known formerly as a WIMP environment, for Windows, icons, mouse and pointer). A pointer (arrow) controlled by the mouse is used to select among graphic windows, icons, buttons and drop-down (or pull-up) menu items; clicking or double-clicking on the mouse button or buttons activates the item selected (starting a program, for example). Most functions can also be activated by keyboard shortcuts, which can be quicker than mouse-clicks once learned, but are not so intuitively obvious for beginners.

Other functions of the OS include formatting floppy disks, copying files between disks and folders and creating new folders. Folders – or directories – are areas of file/document storage into which disks may be divided in a hierarchical manner: folders containing files, more folders (sub-folders) or both.

As well as GUI PCs, text-only 'dumb terminals' may still be encountered, particularly in the context of library catalogues. These have no processing power themselves, being connected by cable to a powerful central computer (or server) which contains the catalogue database, processes all search requests and returns the results to the terminal. With no mouse, all commands have to be entered from the keyboard, but these commands are usually simplified and displayed on screen, especially for library users as distinct from staff. 'Thin clients' are a related technology, but usually have some processing power to drive a GUI screen with mouse as per a normal PC, only the programs are being run on a remote server and just displayed on the client.

Peripheral devices may be attached to PCs: such things as printers, document scanners, external modems (which connect the PC to the phone line) and headphones. These days most PCs in an organization will probably be connected to a network, so a network connection (either cable or wireless) will be used to access these peripherals and the internet. Also worth a mention among peripherals are barcode scanners, which are of especial importance to library IT functions. Special input/output devices may be available for those with physical disabilities.

As well as desktop PCs, mobile computers or laptops may well be encountered, and are even offered for loan in some libraries; although they can run from internal batteries, these have limited power duration and an external power pack to connect to the mains is standard. They may have a touch-pad instead of a mouse, but mice can usually be attached as an optional extra.

Saving, backing-up and floppy disks

Any work carried out on a PC, except the most superficial, will need to be saved to disk. Floppy disks used to be the only option here, but these are now seldom used (Apple Macs no longer come with floppy drives as standard – they are only available as an external optional extra). It is more usual now for work to be saved to the hard disk of the PC or to shared storage space on a network (hard disks on a centralized file server). Frequent saving of your document as you work (at least once every paragraph when word-processing) prevents having to retype pages of data in case of power loss, machine malfunction or program faults. It is much quicker to save to a hard disk, so if you need the data on removable media (which is convenient for transferring data between physically separate computer systems – what Americans call 'SneakerNet'), save to hard disk as you work, and copy from the hard disk when finished (better still, save to a network drive if your system has one; that way, if the PC you're working on should malfunction, you can simply move to a different PC, from which your data on the network drive will be equally accessible).

The most important point to emphasize here is the vital necessity of backing up data; indeed, this can't be overemphasized. Many people, when they first encounter computers, are anxious about accidentally damaging the hardware or software in some way. But apart from such damage being extremely unlikely, these things can always be replaced. What is much more irreplaceable is the data that is entered into the computer: this is the really invaluable, vital component of any computer system. A single copy of a document or database kept on a flimsy floppy disk is extremely vulnerable and open to damage or loss.

If connected to a network, saving to the shared server drives should obviate the need to make a manual back-up; these network drives will be (or certainly should be) backed up themselves every night, on tape drives, recordable/rewritable CD-ROM or DVD, network attached storage (special back-up drives) or even over the internet on the computers of commercial storage providers. The back-up media should be stored off-site in a separate location from the servers themselves, so that even in the event of a disaster such as fire or flood destroying the computer drives, the data will be safe and recoverable once the computers and software are replaced.

Printing and printers

In spite of long-derided predictions of computers leading to the 'paperless office', the introduction of IT has led in fact to more paper being produced than ever before; people seem to prefer studying the information produced by PCs in hard copy form rather than reading it from a screen. This means printing facilities need to be provided, the management of which in a library environment can become complicated.

The main issue to arise is that of charging for printing, to cover the cost of both paper and ink-jet or toner cartridges. Several charging strategies are possible: to leave it free to the user; to have the printer positioned behind the counter so that users have to request their printouts at the counter and can be charged at the same time; to use a card-controlled printing system so that a card has to be swiped through a barcode reader that debits the balance recorded on the magnetic strip on the card (like photocopy cards); or to use a print charging program, which automatically deducts from the user's printing account whenever something is sent to the printer.

Multifunction peripherals (MFPs) may be used instead: as well as printing, these provide facilities for scanning, photocopying and faxing. However they may further complicate the charging situation and the individual functions are probably not as good as with dedicated machines. Photocopying in particular is likely to need a heavy-duty machine in a library, but some of these are now networkable, so can be used as printers by networked PCs.

Other peripherals

Apart from printers, other peripherals which might be found associated with PCs are: document scanners (as distinct from barcode scanners), which can scan images and text for use by a PC, scanning text either as a graphic image or in OCR (optical character recognition) format (this allows the text to be edited as if it had been typed in); CD-ROM drives (but these may not be needed where a CD-ROM network is present, of which more later); and DVD drives. Again, in all but the smallest library setting these devices are more likely to be available over the network than be attached to individual computers.

In addition, specialized equipment may be needed for users with learning and language difficulties or physical disabilities, especially with the current emphasis on social inclusion. This might include special keyboards, tracker balls rather than mice, software to increase the size of the image on the monitor, speech synthesizers to 'read out' what's on screen to those with restricted vision, magnifying copy-holders and so on.

For display and educational purposes, data projectors may be employed where the output from a PC is projected onto an ordinary screen or a special white-board which can be 'drawn' on with a special pen as if it were a mouse. This leaves no physical mark on the board but an electronic trail, as if someone were drawing on the computer screen using a graphics program and the resulting lines were being projected. The pen can also be used as a mouse so that the projected buttons, icons and menu items can be 'clicked' on and the PC will respond accordingly.

Networks

In the early days of computing (of mainframes and minicomputers) all the processing was done by a large central computer with many dumb terminals attached. When the micro came along, it was seen as a release from central control, and represented a huge increase in computing power on individual desktops.

Now these PCs are being linked together again in LANs (local area networks), with a return to some measure of centralized control coupled with a much more efficient use of shared resources. A big difference from the mainframe–terminal model is that the workstations still contain powerful CPUs and therefore don't have to rely on the central server for all the processing, which speeds up processing greatly. However, so-called 'thin clients' are slowly gaining ground in larger organizations: these come somewhere between workstations (or 'fat clients') and dumb terminals, containing enough processing power to run a graphical interface and mouse, but with the applications running on a remote application server and the client providing program output and input.

There is also a half-way house between fat and thin clients: PCs with restricted processing power (perhaps older, near obsolescent machines) which can run some programs or run them from an application server. These clients are sometimes called 'diskless workstations' when no hard or floppy drives are provided, all saving having to be done over the network; the advantage is that PCs with fewer moving parts require less maintenance, and it also prevents users installing or downloading software, or booting from a floppy or CD/DVD. As can be seen there is rather a continuum than a hard-and-fast distinction between these various types of client/workstation, with the precise relationship between PC and network servers being a flexible matter of network policy and management.

Whichever type of client is decided on, to network PCs you need either data cabling to link the components together physically or the installation of wireless access points (WAPs), special networking software installed on the computers (this is usually included with a modern OS) and network cards or wifi (wireless) cards inside each workstation. Wired network cards have sockets which are connected to wall sockets by lengths of cable; longer lengths connect the wall sockets (or 'ports') to central server computers, or to 'hubs' which in turn are connected to servers. Wifi cards just need to be configured to talk to the nearest WAP. Wifi networks have therefore great convenience in needing no wired infrastructure, but are not as reliable or as fast as the best wired networks and have security implications in that anyone with a wifi laptop within range could access your network unless stringent security measures are taken.

There are two main models of computer networking: peer-to-peer and client–server. A peer-to-peer (or P2P) network consists of several PCs linked together and sharing resources: peripherals, software and storage space. In libraries, client–server networking is more the norm: here, many workstation PCs are linked to a very powerful server PC (or several). The workstations can carry out much processing themselves, but the servers enhance the network by offering various centralized functions. They can contain lists of authorized users so that no-one else can log on to the network (access control); they can act as print servers, controlling access to several printers on the network; special servers can run a CD-ROM network; servers with large disk space can act as storage space for users' work; servers run the automated library system; they can control access to other networks, especially the internet; they can provide e-mail services; and application servers can run the actual programs which the PCs display.

Special network operating systems (NOS) were needed for networks in the past, but most modern OSs come with networking built in. Linux especially, with its UNIX inheritance, is a multi-user, multi-tasking operating system with networking capabilities built into its very core; the same software that can be used as an individual home desktop OS can be used as a powerful server OS. Its windowing system especially (X windows – on which the GUIs are built) is intrinsically networkable, with any Linux client able to log on to any other Linux machine on the network, working in effect as a thin client. With the increasing acceptance of other OSs besides those of Microsoft, mixed environments may well be the norm in the future, with Linux servers, for example, providing network services to Microsoft and Apple clients.

Advantages of networking

There are many advantages to a networked system, in the sharing of resources, the pooling of hardware and the provision of security.

By sharing software resources, many users can access a single source of data (like the library catalogue) and save their work to a single secure location on the file server (as mentioned above in relation to back-ups – something that could also be regarded as an aspect of security). The program itself might reside on a server and a workstation might call it from there to run in its own memory; it will probably run faster if it's installed and run on the workstation, but here again a network can make installation faster by distributing the software over the network rather than manually on each PC.

If peripherals such as printers, scanners, CD-ROM drives and so on are also linked to the network, all users on the network can access these devices, and not just the PC to which the device is attached. Or, to look at it another way, you don't need as many of these devices as there are PCs, but only one of each for a certain number of workstations. With a network, peripherals don't have to be connected to an individual PC: they can simply be plugged into a network port and placed in the most convenient or secure location.

From the point of view of security, networked PCs make centralized access control much easier: special servers keep a list of all users who have been given computer accounts, with their passwords, and only users who have an account, and who use the correct password, can log on to any workstation. This means of course that procedures have to be set up to decide who is eligible, what resources on the network they may have access to, how much to charge for such access and allocate accounts. In academic and special libraries the workstations in the library are likely to be part of the LAN of the wider organization, so allocation of user accounts may well be handled by the IT department rather than the library.

Another aspect of security that networking can help with is computer viruses: the virus-checking software can be administered and distributed centrally, so that it's always up to date on every PC. At the same time, networking can increase vulnerability to virus attack by allowing viruses to spread very quickly over network links, rather than being carried physically between machines via floppy disk. This vulnerability has been highlighted recently by high-profile virus attacks carried across the world by e-mail messages. The answer is to keep the anti-virus software up to date and make sure at least one person is monitoring news of virus 'outbreaks' so as to warn people in advance of suspicious e-mail attachments so that they can avoid opening them.

Other sorts of malware are increasingly prevalent besides viruses: spyware is the name for any software which is surreptitiously installed on your PC and records data or key-presses, reporting back to the perpetrator and raising the possibility of identity theft; spam is often spread these days from 'ghost' PCs, which unbeknownst to their owners have been hijacked by the spammers and which relay huge amounts of spam to e-mail addresses all over the world; diallers are also sometimes automatically installed from unscrupulous websites, making internet connections via hugely expensive phone numbers. Any competent network administrator should be able to install systems to prevent this sort of abuse on a networked system.

Another security issue arises where a network is connected to other networks (especially the internet) and concerns the possibility of unauthorized users outside the network hacking into it and destroying or corrupting data or viewing confidential records. This can be prevented with firewalls: hardware and software that sits between the LAN and the outside world and prevents such unauthorized intrusion.

There may still be a place for a standalone PC even in a predominantly networked environment (quite apart from very small outlets and those libraries without a physical network infrastructure). For example, there may be a need to allow for access to basic software by the casual user who doesn't have time to wait for a computer account to be created (though 'guest' logons on the network can get round that problem). Or more controlled access to printing resources might be achieved by having a single printer attached to a standalone PC, so that users have to take their work to this PC via floppy disk. Control and charging can still be achieved on standalones by having PCs accessible by swipe-card: a barcode reader attached to each PC would have to validate each user's card (and their associated PIN) before they could log on, and the associated software would deduct time from the account they've pre-paid for, or only allow access for the time left on the card.

Intranets

An intranet is basically a mini-internet based on a LAN – that is, pages of purely local information can be accessed by everyone with a network account. The pages, or a selection from them, may also be made available to the wider internet (these publicly accessible pages sometimes being referred to as the extranet). The internet, e-mails and web pages are discussed in more detail later in this chapter.

An intranet allows local communication of more permanent information than would be appropriate to e-mails, and a local form of information retrieval. Ideally, the library should have a presence on any such intranet (for example, an academic library should have a presence on the intranet of its parent institution), with the sort of information previously only available on printed library guides (opening hours, rules and regulations, plans and locations of material/resources, basic instructions and so forth). Application forms can also be made available: for printing out so that they can be filled in manually, or for copying to disk so that they can be completed on screen and e-mailed to the appropriate recipient.

There is great potential for more extensive information access, as any special indexes, reading lists, subject guides, etc. can be included; there is also scope for library promotion – promotion on the intranet can be seen as an electronic extension of the traditional hard-copy library display.

Wider community information is also the type of material for which an intranet is ideal. Larger libraries may even have digitization projects whereby collections are scanned into computers and the texts made available online via the intranet.

Software

The software programs (also called applications or packages) that are available for PCs are many and various. Here are some of the more common types:

1 **Word-processing packages** (WPs) are used to produce documents of all sorts (whether ultimately printed out or not): letters, reports, memos, theses, etc. As these WPs have got more powerful over the years, they have incorporated some of the features of desktop publishing (DTP: see below) and graphics packages, with the inclusion of display typefaces, small pictures or 'clip-art', borders, etc. They can also now include tables like those formerly only found in spreadsheet programs. To copy data between different WPs, many programs allow you to save in the format of other programs, but you can always use the plain text option (ASCII – American Standard Code for Information Interchange, pronounced 'askey') or Rich Text Format (RTF), which saves some of the formatting. PDF (Portable Document Format) is also an option on some WPs – this is the format for Adobe Acrobat Reader and is convenient for circulating a non-editable document, whereby people can read the document but not change it.

2 **Spreadsheets** are for the entry and manipulation of numerical data. Columns of numbers (amounts of money, for example) can be entered and the program can add them up (or manipulate them in some other way) automatically. If any of the numbers are changed, the total can be recalculated instantly. Spreadsheets are obviously of use for budgetary data, statistics and so on, but can also be used for presenting textual data in columnar form, though WPs can now do this too. Specialist accounting packages are more likely to be used by finance departments, but spreadsheets are fine for personal finances.

3 **Databases** are used to record any collection of information, and in their most basic or 'flat-file' form are made up of a collection of records (like catalogue cards) where each record is divided into a number of 'fields', each containing an individual item of information. The most obvious example is the library's database of books and other items,

where each title comprises an individual record with individual fields like author, publisher, date and so on (actually, a library catalogue would be in a more sophisticated or 'relational' form as explained later in this chapter). Information can be displayed one record at a time, in catalogue card fashion, or like a spreadsheet, with each row representing a single record and each column one of the fields; this latter view allows information in the fields to be compared easily and columns of numerical data to be manipulated, and makes interchange of information with spreadsheets easier.

4 **Graphics packages** are used to produce visual displays or output; pictures can be scanned in or imported from remote sources, manipulated and have text added. Such packages are often used with DTP.

5 **Desktop publishing** (DTP) software is used to amalgamate text from a WP and pictures from a graphics package to produce high-quality publishable output for pamphlets, brochures, leaflets, advertisements, posters and even full-length books. It can be used for library publications, user guides, guidance or promotions, but in a larger organization a specialist graphics/marketing department will take care of this (probably using Apple Macs, the favoured PC of graphic designers).

6 **Presentation** packages allow the user to create 'slides' of information which can be printed on acetate to form OHP slides or projected directly from a data projector linked to the PC.

7 **Web creation** tools are for making pages for a website on the internet, of which more later.

8 **Web browsers** are the clients for the world wide web, allowing access to websites and other internet information; this also will be expanded on later.

9 **Groupware** is a general term for networkable collaboration software; this can be invaluable for management processes, allowing users to work together online, using such things as shared calendars, diaries, project planners and e-mail.

E-mail (electronic mail)

E-mail is a way of sending typed-in messages to and from people with PCs attached to networks (including telecommunications networks – the phone line). On a network with its own e-mail server messages can be sent to and from people with e-mail accounts on the LAN, just using the person's name as the e-mail address (a list of names will be stored in the e-mail software as an address list). To send messages to people on other networks or with standalone PCs you'll need to know their full e-mail address (e.g. alanhornsey@01823.com), but frequently used addresses can be stored in a personal address list.

As well as sending and receiving straightforward text messages, you can send files by attaching them to an e-mail – longer documents, picture files or even programs. But once you have an e-mail account you have to make a habit of checking it regularly (at least once every day); otherwise LAN e-mails can become full of unread messages, taking up valuable storage space, while internet e-mail providers usually close down an account which isn't used for some period of time (typically, three months).

It's also a good idea to save copies of outgoing e-mails; breakdowns of communication can happen for all sorts of reasons, and it's vital to have a copy of the e-mail to re-send rather than trying to remember what you wrote. Brief messages should be typed straight in to the e-mail message space, but choose the 'save outgoing message' option if it's of any importance; longer documents can be enclosed as attachments; and messages of intermediate length could be typed into a WP first then copied and pasted into the e-mail message space. E-mails can be sent as HTML documents (the web file format, of which more later), but it is a security risk to read HTML e-mails as malware code can easily be concealed in this way.

'Spamming' can also be a problem, especially in an educational setting. This is where an unsolicited, irrelevant, trivial or even offensive e-mail is sent indiscriminately to everyone on an address list; disciplinary measures may be needed as part of a policy to guard against this.

PCs can now interact with fax machines, and special fax software can also be used to send or receive fax documents, from PC to fax or fax to PC. For PC-to-PC communication there is not much to choose between e-mail and electronic fax – pictures can be included in e-mails as attachments.

Practical IT management

All libraries today should have an IT strategy to guide medium- to long-term planning. This should conform to the larger organization's overall IT strategy and mission statement; it should be open to revision in light of developments in technology, professional practice, government initiatives and socio-economic change. It will lay down the overall direction of IT development and cover such matters as:

- major investments, infrastructure and changes to buildings to accommodate IT layout
- overall responsibility for IT and demarcation of tasks between IT staff and library staff
- sources for hardware/software, the tendering process and financial auditing procedures
- legal requirements: health and safety legislation, the Data Protection Act, the Disability Discrimination Act
- the nature and extent of a web presence
- marketing, promotion, community information and publicity for new services/programs
- the balance between print, CD-ROM and electronic sources of information.

An IT policy may be a separate document or series of documents to cover short- to medium-term contingencies as devolved from the overall strategy. This would cover such areas as:

- staff induction and continuing staff development
- user education
- continuous updating of software
- a rolling programme of hardware renewal
- standardization of printed output (according to the organization's house style)
- maintenance requirements
- charges for IT use and/or printing
- whether a booking system is needed
- how to ensure copyright and software licensing restrictions are adhered to.

Procedures should be available in printed form as well as electronically for immediate reference and staff training. Updatable whenever IT changes take place, these would describe the precise method of carrying out IT tasks, as decided in the IT policy.

Location

Some consideration needs to be given to the physical layout of IT resources. Sufficient network cabling and power sockets should be planned for as a matter of course. Space for each computer has to take into account the room needed for mice and mouse mats, and for each user's paperwork and copyholders. Allowance also needs to be made for seats to be pulled in and out and for people to be able to pass between tables or desks when seating is fully occupied; the seats themselves should comply with health and safety criteria.

User education

While formal programmes of user education may be in place (especially in academic libraries), all library staff should know the basics of how to get users started on the IT systems: how to log on if a network is used (and how to apply for a network account in the first place), where the main programs are to be found in the menuing system, how to format disks, save work and back-up, how to print out work, how to spell-check, and so on. An outline of user guides should also be provided, giving the location of WP or DTP templates in the library's house style.

Problems/troubleshooting/fault reporting

This covers the simplest and most frequent types of problem that users encounter, and in effect overlaps with user induction and education. It includes such things as checking cables are connected, changing toner and paper in printers, clearing paper jams in same, checking compatibility of disks and/or versions of programs and the like. Many software problems can be overcome by closing and re-opening programs, logging off and back on or even restarting (or rebooting) the computer. You should ensure all work is saved before such attempts are made (this may not be possible if the computer is totally frozen, 'locked up' or 'hung'). It may be at this level of problem that IT technicians need to be contacted; procedures should be laid down as to when IT faults need reporting, to whom, and whether and how they should be recorded.

Booking systems and charges

If booking systems are used, the method should be explained in detail to users. These systems can get very complicated, but may be essential if demand is high and resources limited. Systems include dividing the day into hour or even half-hour slots, which people book in advance; decisions have to be made as to whether to limit the total time or the number of consecutive slots people can book, to fix how far in advance such bookings can be made, whether penalties should be incurred for not taking up booked sessions and how long to wait before freeing a slot if someone doesn't turn up. The system can be manual or on computer, but in this case a manual system may well be more suitable, as the actual book can be consulted at the counter instantly if all computers are in use. Where charging is used, the amounts and valid methods of payment have to be specified: it may be by cash in advance, by pre-paid account or by pre-charged swipe-cards. Printing charges may likewise be paid in cash at the counter, by pre-paid accounts held on the network or via a swipe-card system similar to that used with photocopiers. Consumables such as floppy disks or recordable/rewritable CDs/DVDs may be offered for sale at the library counter; charges for these should also be detailed.

Security

People need to keep their passwords secret so that network integrity can be maintained, and this point should be stressed to users. Student users in particular have a habit of revealing their passwords to each other and allowing others to log on to their account. This practice should be strongly discouraged, and penalties may have to be considered if the abuse continues.

Computer viruses also threaten network security and are an ever-present menace now they are commonly spread by e-mail. Virus-checking software should be installed and kept up to date on all machines, though this is more likely to be handled by IT network staff; if a virus is detected, the machine should be kept off limits until it can be examined by IT staff. The precise procedures to follow should be documented, including who to contact in the event of a virus warning.

Discipline

Following on from abuse of passwords, unacceptable behaviour may well be an issue that needs addressing in school or college libraries. Mobile phones are the latest nuisance to afflict libraries, though not one restricted to the use of IT; but IT areas must have similar rules to the rest of the library as to whether mobile phones are permitted at all, or whether the user has to leave the library in order to use them. Similar considerations apply to the use of personal stereos, and whether to ban them outright or tolerate them if the volume is kept down. More IT-specific problems are the playing of computer games and overuse of chat rooms; if these are banned, the ban has to be enforced by constant monitoring, and possibly by the imposition of penalties (such as removing network access for a period) if dissuasion is ineffective. Sending spam e-mails and attempting to hack into secure parts of the network are other activities that may call for such sanctions. Accessing or downloading objectionable content from the internet such as porn may also need dealing with: written guidelines should be prepared in advance, and it may be that the use of website blocking software will need to be considered.

Integrated library systems

Perhaps the most fundamental item of IT in any library, an integrated library system (ILS) will contain a database of the library's holdings, which can be manipulated in many ways to facilitate and enhance the basic library functions of:

* cataloguing
* circulation of loanable material (loans, returns, reservations, fines and letters)
* accessing the library's stock (using online public access catalogues or OPACs)
* acquisition of material
* interlibrary loans (ILLs)
* organization of periodicals.

Such systems are available from many suppliers in many different configurations, from 'made-to-measure' bespoke systems to 'off-the-peg' turnkey systems. Well-known vendors are Dynix (Horizon), Ex-Libris (Aleph), Fretwell-Downing (OLIB), Geac, IS-Oxford (Heritage IV), Innovative, Sirsi and Talis. Open source ILS are under development and some are being piloted in a small number of libraries, the most developed being Koha from New Zealand; as with all OSS one advantage is that it is freely downloadable to examine and evaluate (from www.koha.org).

ILS are being developed and upgraded all the time to take advantage of new technology and advances in the wider IT world and to secure competitive advantage. Most suppliers will offer to supply hardware as well as software, but you will probably find cheaper sources of hardware. A maintenance contract (software only or including hardware where that's part of the package) is a standard part of the purchase.

Most systems offer a choice between using text-only terminals to access information on the server and using special client software on a normal PC. The latter approach has the advantage that other programs can also be used on the PC, making it more efficient in utilizing hardware and available space. On the other hand, where demand for computing resources is high you could end up with all public-access PCs being used for other purposes and none being available to search the library catalogue. In such a case dedicated terminals are invaluable; otherwise, some PCs will need to be reserved for library catalogue use, either via software which prevents any other programs from being used, or by their being placed close to the counter, reference desk or other service point where library staff can monitor use.

Whichever sort of system is employed, procedures should be put in place for temporary manual systems to take over in the event of power failure, maintenance downtime or unpredictable system crashes.

Cataloguing

The digital electronic catalogue lies at the heart of any automated library system; it is the basic database used by every other function. As a 'relational' database it will in fact consist of multiple databases, with the main catalogue record being in effect a series of 'links' to other databases (title database, author database, publisher database, etc.), so that any particular author, publisher or whatever only has to be entered once.

The bibliographic data can be entered manually via keyboard or records may be downloaded from online bibliographic sources available from publishers, library suppliers or other commercial services; alternatively, the data might be transferred from an order record where acquisitions modules are used. ISBNs (automatically validated) can be used to identify records, or unique record numbers can be automatically generated by the system. When converting from a manual system, a professional data-entry service will probably be needed to transfer card catalogues into electronic form.

Special data or terms may be entered for each item to facilitate information retrieval and printing of specialized lists of material. Different types of material (books, tapes, discs, maps, etc.) can be distinguished in each record, and different fields used for different types (e.g. running time for tapes, directors instead of authors for films, etc.). Also, subject terms (descriptors) or keywords will need to be entered for each record if subject searching is to be used; this will entail compiling a local thesaurus to ensure consistency between records and descriptors, and needs to be continually monitored to be effective.

Circulation control

Each title record can have several copy (or accession) records linked to it, as it's the individual copy of any title that can be borrowed, and the accession record contains the information about loan period and restrictions. Each accession record has a unique accession number, which is usually recorded on the physical item in the form of a barcode (library suppliers can supply items with barcodes already attached as part of their processing service); the details can then be swiped in at the issue counter and the loan/return of that item recorded. So a single title record can have several accession records associated with it of varying loan periods for various types of borrower, or even no loan period at all for reference copies.

Complications can ensue with some items like video or audio tapes where more than one programme is on a single tape; then you have a single physical item to loan, but two or more titles on the item – the precise reverse of the situation with books (single title with multiple physical copies). Not every contingency that might arise can be predicted in any system, so ad hoc procedures may have to be devised for these unforeseen situations as and when they arise, bearing in mind the overall policies concerning consistency and convenience.

In the case of tapes with multiple titles, it may be that only the first title has an associated accession record (which identifies the physical item that can be borrowed), while the other title records contain an indicator that directs searchers to the title that has the circulation information attached. For example, instead of listing an author (not really appropriate for tapes), the author field might contain a tape number; this is useful when tapes are stored, as is usually the case, in non-public-access areas in number order and therefore have to be requested by number. The users will need to be told that if a tape record has no circulation information at all (i.e. no accession record), they will have to search by the tape number to find the title record which does have such information attached, if they want to know whether the tape's on loan or not. Of course they can always take a chance and just ask for that tape number anyway; the counter staff can soon tell them if it is available. This gives some idea of the sorts of practical (if not ideal) 'work-arounds' that sometimes have to be devised for unforeseen (and unforeseeable) circumstances.

As well as a database of loanable items, the system will need a database of borrowers, with varying degrees of detail (name and address at least). Whenever personal information is stored on computer (or otherwise) the provisions of the Data Protection Act become relevant, the most important of which are that personal details are not to be divulged to anyone else, but that the person whose details are recorded may always examine his or her own record, and that they must be informed how the information is to be used. Some proof of identity and of address will be needed, for overdue letters if nothing else. You can have different types of borrower (e.g. child/adult, staff/student) with different loan rules (total number of items on loan, number of any particular category of material, default duration of loan, etc.). If the library is part of a larger organization, you may be able to download records from the MIS (management information system) maintained by the administrative staff; this represents a huge saving of library staff time.

Again, barcode numbers will probably be used as a unique personal identifier; the barcode is usually included on the borrower's card (this can be a dual library/staff/student card if the library is part of a larger organization). This means that two swipes of a barcode (on item and on borrower card) are all that's needed to loan an item. The return date is calculated automatically by the system according to the pre-set circulation rules for that category of material and that type of borrower (though this date can be overridden and a date entered manually); to return an item only a single swipe of the item's barcode is needed.

The circulation system is also used to record reservation requests and generate letters and fines. If an item is reserved on computer, when it's returned a message appears on screen to this effect so that the item can be put aside, and a letter generated to the requester to collect the item. Overdue letters are also automatically generated, and fines calculated if items are not returned as per overdue letter; the system can also apply a block on further loans if items are not returned or fines not paid. Again, the number of reservations allowed, the frequency and wording of letters, and the amount and frequency of fines, can be made to vary with type of borrower.

Fines and letters are usually generated by the system as part of an overnight program; the queue of letters is then printed out next morning on demand. The various rules can get very complicated, with variable open/closed days, multiple types of borrower and multiple categories of loanable material, each with different rules for each type of borrower. A printed table of types of user and categories of material will probably be found essential.

Online public access catalogues

To access the system's database of library stock, the library user employs an online public access catalogue (OPAC) terminal (either a dumb terminal or a workstation as explained above). Library staff can use the OPAC interface as well, of course, but they also have the option of interrogating the database using the catalogue module directly. Some at least of the bibliographic details entered at the cataloguing stage are now available for searches, the system usually giving the option of what fields to search on.

As well as the standard author and/or title search, a user might be able to search for material using specific subject terms (as long as these are entered at the cataloguing stage, as mentioned above), a keyword from the title (so no special subject terms need be entered), a classification number (presuming some familiarity with the classification scheme) or even a free text search (searching all fields in the catalogue record for the term entered). ISBN searches are also possible.

The catalogue may be made available on CD-ROM or as a web page on the organization's intranet, or even to the general public on the internet. The web page option has the great advantage that the catalogue can be searched wherever there is a workstation, not just in the library. If circulation information is included, the potential borrower doesn't have to visit the library if s/he knows the item is out on loan, but can still reserve the item by phone or even from the terminal.

The details of a title are displayed after a successful search, plus the relevant circulation details of the physical copies: the location where they're to be found (possibly a remote site), the class mark and/or shelf mark, the loan period and whether they're available or already on loan (if the latter, when they're due back). Some systems allow users to reserve items on loan from an OPAC, for which they'll need a unique PIN to access their loan record.

Although online catalogues have largely replaced card catalogues, lists of special items can still be made available in hard-copy form by the selective printing of portions of the catalogue – for example, student reading lists, or lists of items which are not normally browsable on the open access shelves (video tapes for example). A printed subject index to the class numbers will be invaluable for subject searching, and a periodical index may be necessary (though often periodicals aren't included on the electronic catalogue anyway, so the index will need to be printed some other way).

Acquisitions

Most systems include the option of an acquisitions module, but this is not always employed when the library is part of a larger organization, as the finance department may have its own automated system which must be used. Whichever system is used must be consistent with the fiscal and auditing policies of the organization.

Where an acquisitions module is used, basic bibliographic data for an item (plus edition, price and number of copies) can be entered manually on the order record or downloaded from an electronic source – possibly one specially provided by the library supplier. This record will later form the basis of the catalogue record when the item arrives and is added to stock. The system can print out a hard copy of the order ready for sending to the supplier, but increasingly the trend is to send the order electronically via e-mail, fax, the internet or a direct online link.

When items arrive, receipts and invoice payments are added; the system may automatically assign these to cost centres, or print/display them against budget headings. The system should advise of ordered but overdue items, so users can be warned of delay and suppliers chased (again via hard-copy letter or electronic communication).

Interlibrary loans

This is another optional extra, not always purchased with the rest of the system. Requests may be printed out or sent electronically, the system tracking the stage the request has got to, so the requester can be kept up to date. Any special loan conditions can be included, and warnings generated if an item becomes overdue for return.

For British Library loans, coupon numbers can be quoted in the electronic request so payment is made at the same time. Requests can also be made electronically through the BL's Automated Request Transmission service (ART), which is briefly described later in this chapter.

Periodicals

Journals are very complicated to keep track of due to their often irregular issue periods, so again the periodical module is an optional extra on most systems, which many libraries dispense with. There are other specialist computerized periodical systems not connected to integrated library systems, and the library may choose to use one of these.

Details entered into any periodical system should include journal title, ISSN, previous titles and the expected date of publication or arrival of the next issue. In theory the system should be able to predict this last item based on the previous history of publication dates, but the notorious unreliability of journal publication can easily upset this, hence the related chasing facility (overseas journals in particular may arrive at the library some months behind the official publication date).

If the module is part of an integrated system, then subscription costs may be allocatable to the cost centres of the acquisitions module. Another advantage is that titles will be searchable on OPACs; otherwise, databases must be made searchable as a separate package, or a hard copy of journal holdings must be printed out.

Individual journal copies may be assigned to various physical locations and, if the library is part of a larger organization, there may need to be a circulation list for titles which are distributed to individuals before being returned to the library. It may also be the case that some titles (especially newspapers) are purchased as printed items but archived in electronic form (e.g. CD-ROM); the system should be able to include this information.

Information retrieval
Optical discs (CD-ROM, DVD)

CDs and DVDs can both be used for information storage as well as for music or movies; a CD-ROM (read-only memory) looks identical to an audio CD, but instead of music it contains several types of digital information (text, pictures, moving images and sound), which can only be read by a CD-ROM or DVD player connected to a PC (CD-ROM drives can also play audio CDs, but CD players can't read CD-ROMs). DVD (digital versatile disc) has become tremendously popular as a distribution medium for film and TV, but is also used for data storage: while a CD-ROM can hold up to 650Mb of information, a DVD has a maximum capacity of 4.7Gb (Gigabytes: 1 Gb = 1000Mb, or about a billion bytes) per side and can be double-sided, unlike CD-ROMs. A 'double-layer' DVD can contain 8.5Gb per side, hence a massive 17Gb per disc, about 26 times the capacity of a CD-ROM. This means that databases which were previously only available on multiple-CD sets can now be provided on one or two DVDs. Both CD-ROMs and DVDs will be referred to here as ODs (optical discs – optical because they're read with laser lightbeams).

ODs can also be used for information storage in their R or RW incarnations (recordable – can only be written to once; re-writable – can be overwritten several times). This requires special R or RW drives that can 'burn' information onto the discs as well as read them, but these come as standard on most modern PCs, making these discs very convenient for off-site back-up and archival purposes. They are also commonly used for application distribution, programs generally being far too big to fit on floppy disks any more.

In the early days of CD-ROM the discs were normally accessed on standalone PCs, each containing its own CD-ROM player; the discs were often stored behind the counter for safe keeping and had to be requested by the user. Increasingly, OD networks are being employed, so that the individual user may never see the actual disc, but clicks on an icon or selects an item from a menu on the workstation. This greatly increases the security of expensive discs.

The actual disc will be stored in a computer room, possibly permanently in an OD 'tower' attached to the network, in a 'juke box' or 'pre-cached' onto a hard disk. The tower approach (basically just a stack of OD players in a single box) is expensive and takes up a lot of space. The juke box (a box with one or several OD players and many discs) is also expensive, but takes up less space per disc. It can be slower as the user has to wait for a particular disc to be mechanically loaded into one of the players, but is useful for the really big sets of CDs that are not available on DVD.

The pre-caching approach is becoming the standard. The information on a disc is downloaded onto a server's hard disk as an OD 'image'; special software then 'fools' the PC into treating this image as if it were an actual disc in a player. As the price of hard discs keeps falling, this is a relatively inexpensive way of storing the information, and as hard disks are much faster to access than OD players, access for users is faster as well. The only thing to make sure of is that the database producer's licence doesn't forbid downloading to hard disk. Networking software may also include a number of features that facilitate the management of the system: a menuing system so that the organization of the discs is made easier; a feature allowing you to specify the number of concurrent users, thus keeping within licence conditions; and a program that makes usage statistics available.

'Search engine' software is needed to access the data on the disc; this is usually included on the OD, in which case it may run directly from the disc, but sometimes on floppy disk or disks (in which case it will need to be installed on the PC). Again OD networking can simplify the installation of search engines, either by placing them on the server from which workstations can run them, or by distributing the search engines to each individual workstation over the network. OD networking software can simplify this task by compressing the search engine files into a single 'zipped' file, which is downloaded to a PC the first time the disc is selected from that workstation; the file is then decompressed or 'unzipped' and the search engine files are copied to the PC hard disk, all of which takes place automatically without the user having to be aware of it (or transparently to the end-user, as IT jargon has it).

Unfortunately, search engines are invariably different for each disc, although there may be 'families' of discs with the same interface (such as the SilverPlatter search engine), so library staff have no option but to familiarize themselves with the basics of several programs (and the information on the databases) by constant practice and updating.

The sort of information on these discs varies tremendously, from relatively straightforward databases of bibliographic information (BookBank, BNB – another source of machine-readable catalogue data for library cataloguing) and periodical indexes or abstracting services, to full-text information (newspapers, encyclopaedias). User education will be needed not just to show searchers how to use the interface, but to inform them of the nature of the data on each disc and let them know that not everything is full text which can be printed out straight away, but may need to be ordered through the ILL system.

As well as databases, information in other forms may be available on OD, as well as full-blown programs (especially educational programs in an academic context). Again this all has serious implications for user education and library inductions: there can be hundreds of ODs on a single network. As well as demonstrating the search engine and pointing out the program's 'help' facility, it may be a good idea to produce printed reference guides or help cards for some at least of the less intuitive titles, and also lists of journals covered by indexing and abstracting discs (many producers include such cards and lists amongst their documentation).

Many titles take advantage of the multimedia facilities of modern PCs, so provision will need to be made for those that include sound. Usually loudspeakers are disabled or removed and headphones made available from behind the library counter; ideally it should be possible to plug more than one set into the PC to allow for shared sessions.

With pre-caching and special OD networking software, it's not just genuine discs that can be treated in this way; any software, document or database can be pre-cached and treated as if it were located on an OD. Therefore, these 'pseudo-discs' can contain locally generated information and full-scale programs; in fact the OD menuing system could be used as the main access point for all the software on the network.

The information on some discs is available in dual format, with hard copy and disc available – and there may be an internet source of the same information available as well – so decisions may have to be made about which format is right for purchase/subscription. Where the title is available both in disc form and on the internet, the two might be able to interact; for example, an encyclopaedia on DVD might be able to download updates to its articles from the encyclopaedia's website.

Sometimes if a hard-copy format is purchased, the associated OD will be included free, or vice versa. However, if a choice has to be made, the pros and cons of OD access as compared with hard copy and online sources will have to be considered.

Advantages of optical discs

* A single database is accessible to multiple users at the same time (subject to licence restrictions).
* ODs are accessible across the network, not just in the library.
* The discs take up far less space than hard copy.
* Many users are more ready to use PCs than reference books.
* Many search strategies are possible; users are not reliant on a single index.
* Searching is faster with an OD than with printed versions.
* The discs are quality-controlled.
* Staff become expert users.
* LAN connections are faster than most online connections.
* ODs are more reliable than the internet – less downtime than over telecommunication links.
* Search software may be tailor-made for the data, rather than generic – an advantage over the internet.

Disadvantages of optical discs

- PCs take up a lot of space (but they can be multi-use, not just ODs).
- OD use needs special equipment/training.
- The capital costs of equipment are high (but again, there are many uses).
- If the library is using standalones, or has only a single-user licence, the OD will be available to only one user at a time.
- OD archives don't reach as far back in time as printed forms.
- They require much more user education.
- Some users are more comfortable with books than IT.
- ODs can be less up to date than online sources.
- Different search engines require more user education than generic web searching.
- Multi-disc sets may be awkward to search, especially across the whole database.

It is also worth bearing in mind that it is perfectly possible to produce ODs of the library's catalogue, once it is in digital format, from the automated library system, using R and RW drives. These discs could then be distributed to any interested parties; the disadvantage is that they will need regular updating as the library's holdings constantly change, and they will not contain circulation information. Therefore it is preferable if the library catalogue can be accessed over the LAN as an extension of the OPACs or as web pages on the intranet.

It is technically possible for a library's OD network to be searchable over the internet, but there are licensing issues here and probably only a subset could be made accessible. The library may need to negotiate with individual database producers over licensing deals; attitudes vary from one publisher to another.

Online services

Most people now probably think of online information services in terms of the internet and free websites, and indeed the sheer amount of information available from that source has mushroomed spectacularly in recent years. However, quantity doesn't imply quality and subscription-based online services are still to be found where accurate, up-to-date, fast, high-quality, in-depth information is needed. Such virtues don't come cheap and therefore are more likely to be used in special libraries and information centres. A business library might subscribe to FT Discovery (now Lexis-Nexis Executive), for example, a legal library to LexisNexis itself, or a medical library to MEDLINE; research centres are other users of such services. The services may charge for connected time or by a yearly subscription charge, which might amount to several thousand pounds a year.

Not long ago these specialized subscription services were only accessible over telecommunications links like Telnet, but increasingly they are being made available over the internet, using a web browser interface, but requiring usernames and passwords to ensure that only subscribers can log on. This demonstrates the convergence that is taking place on the internet, with previously disparate services all becoming accessible via a web browser. The take-up of broadband internet access has also to some extent neutralized the speed advantage of Telnet, and the flexibility of Telnet interfaces has been adapted for web browser use.

Many services however are still accessible via Telnet connections whereby, instead of just requesting files from a remote computer, you actually log on to the 'host' as a regular user. So, as with the web version, you need to register with the host's suppliers and get a user ID and password to log on; the privileges paid for in the service subscription determine which database and how much of it you can access. This system dates from 1974 and was common on UNIX networks before GUIs were in use: as such it still uses a text-only interface where the PC is in effect emulating a dumb terminal on the host computer's network. Some of these services include document delivery – that is, delivery of printed hard copy via the post as well as electronic delivery.

Of particular interest to librarians is the Automated Request Transmission (ART) service of the BLDSC, an electronic adjunct of the normal ILL service. There are several methods of using ART: via third-party online database hosts that offer document delivery, by fax (FAX-line), by the world wide web (ARTWeb), by e-mail (ARTEmail) and by telecommunications (ARTTel). ARTTel itself can be accessed in several different ways: using Telnet, via the internet, by Dialplus or by direct dial (Dialplus, unlike direct dial, involves calling a local 'node' so that you only pay for a local phone call).

However, even ARTTel is accessible via the web, with a browser interface to Telnet: ARTTel using this web browser method is distinct from ARTWeb. With ARTWeb you can only send one request at a time by filling in a web-based template, whereas with ARTTel (however you access it) you link directly with the automated request system in an interactive session where your PC is in effect a terminal of the BLDSC host computer;

hundreds of requests can be sent at the same time this way, by your typing them out beforehand in a text editor and pasting them into the ARTTel screen.

Advantages of online sources

- They are accessible across the network, not just in the library.
- Many search strategies are possible; users are not reliant on a single index.
- Searching is faster with online sources than with printed versions.
- The services are quality-controlled.
- Staff become expert users.
- Search software is tailor-made for the data.
- Sources are constantly updated.
- They can include specialist sources not available from any other source.
- Dedicated 'leased lines' are more reliable than general telecomm links.

Disadvantages of online sources

- Special training in search software is needed.
- They can be expensive.
- Archives don't reach as far back in time as printed forms.
- They may only be accessible via staff, owing to the expense and/or training needed.
- Links are slower than pre-cached ODs over a LAN.
- The links are less reliable than a LAN.

The internet and the web

The internet (or sometimes just 'the net') and the world wide web (www or 'the web') have revolutionized information retrieval over the last couple of decades; all libraries can access sources which would have been unthinkable not long ago, new sources of information have mushroomed, new ways of accessing old sources have been developed, and digital libraries and digitized collections of previously text-only collections have appeared.

The internet is basically just a very large collection of computers, and computer networks, from all over the world, linked together through the telecommunications networks. The information contained on all these computers is available mostly for free, though there is sometimes a charge for password-protected premium services; but the cost of linking to them is very low as only a local phone-line charge has to be paid. There is no single owner or controller of the internet, which has led to a system with masses of information but with little organization.

Many have welcomed this anarchic freedom, but it has implications for the information professional concerning the validity, currency, quality and retrievability of information. The fact has to be faced that there is much that is worthless on the internet, and there is a real challenge to differentiate the wheat from the chaff (and finding all the wheat, not just a small part of it). The downside of internet freedom is that there is much to be found in cyberspace (as the collection of information is sometimes known) that is offensive to many people (if not actually illegal – e.g. pornography/racism).

To log on to the internet a PC is required (though web-enabled mobile phones and TVs are also available); if the PC is standalone, a modem (internal or external) connected to the phone line is also required, plus an account with an ISP (internet service provider), and to access the web you'll need the appropriate web browser software (e.g. Internet Explorer, Mozilla Firefox or Opera). If your PC is connected to a network you'll probably just need to click on the appropriate icon or menu option, as the chances are the network will have been connected to the internet by the IT department.

Links in the recent past could be slow (owing to restricted bandwidth and the amount of network traffic fighting for space on limited telecommunications resources), but the increasing use of broadband connections (about ten times faster than dial-up) has largely overcome this problem in institutional settings. If connections to the internet are through a network (via a proxy/web server and firewall to protect against hacking into local networks) the link can be lost for everyone if there are any problems with the servers, or routine maintenance or upgrading is required. A web proxy server can save or 'cache' the pages passing through it so those pages are still searchable even when the internet connection is down.

Although many people think that the internet and the web are synonymous, strictly speaking the web is just one of several services available over the internet. Other parts of the internet are:

- **Chat**: instant textual communication between several participants via a virtual 'chat room'

- **Usenet**: BBS (bulletin board system) is used to post messages on discussion forums (newsgroups)
- **FTP** (file transfer protocol): file exchange between internet-connected computers
- **Telnet**: logging on to a remote server as a client machine of that computer
- **Gopher**: internet document searching system
- **Instant messaging**: sending brief messages to other PCs more quickly than e-mail
- **VOIP**: voice over IP (internet protocol) – free phone calls to other subscribers.

However, all these services are now accessible via a web browser-based interface as part of the convergence noted previously, so the web and the internet are becoming synonymous in spite of the original distinction. The two main aspects of the internet which library staff will need to deal with are e-mail and the web itself.

E-mail

One of the original reasons for the existence of the internet was its provision of electronic mail, the sending of messages to other users with e-mail addresses. There are two main types of e-mail currently used: POP3 (post office protocol) client–server systems and web-based e-mail.

Dedicated e-mail client software (e.g. Outlook, Mozilla Thunderbird) is normally used to access the POP3 system, where incoming messages are collected by an e-mail server (either on the internet or part of the LAN) and downloaded onto the user's PC when the client connects to the server. Messages are downloaded onto the hard disk, so they can be read later whether the PC is connected to the server or not. The messages can be deleted from the server as soon as they're downloaded or left as duplicates for some specified period of time (say, a week or two). LAN e-mail servers don't have to be connected to the internet at all to send messages from one LAN user to another, though of course the server will need a connection to forward e-mails to addresses outside the LAN.

Web browsers can now interact with these POP3 systems to some extent, but they can also access the web-based e-mail systems (like Hotmail, Yahoo!Mail and Lycos Communication), where messages are stored permanently on a remote internet server. You can only read the e-mails while you're online, though the text can of course be copied and pasted to a local document. The advantage of web-based systems is that you can access them from any computer, anywhere in the world where there's an internet connection; the disadvantage used to be the limited amount of storage space offered, whereas POP3 is limited only by the storage capacity of your hard disk, but recent increases in these limits (e.g. for free services: 250Mb Hotmail; 1Gb Yahoo!; 300Mb Lycos UK) has largely overcome this failing. Of course, there's no reason why you can't have more than one e-mail account using different systems.

When using an internet e-mail service it's a good idea to choose the option that allows you to filter out unwanted junk mail and/or prevent your e-mail address from appearing on general directories; otherwise you may be swamped with unwanted and possibly offensive/pornographic junk e-mails. Security is also now a vital issue with e-mail as most viruses are spread this way. That you should use anti-virus software goes without saying, but you should also ideally not look at HTML e-mails as executable code can be hidden in HTML (there should be an option to look just at the source code), and you should only open attachments from trusted sources, because virus software is often sent as attachments. You might also want to consider changing your e-mail client if you use Outlook; it is known to have many security issues and something like Mozilla Thunderbird should be much safer.

The web

The web consists of computers holding pages of data in HTML (HyperText Mark-up Language) format which can be read by web browser software. As well as information, the pages can contain hypertext links (or 'hyperlinks', or just 'links') which, when clicked on, go straight to a different part of the page, retrieve a different page from that site or go directly to a page at a completely different site.

When a web browser is opened it may open on a favourite web page by default, or perhaps a page of the organization's intranet. The opening page of a site is called its home page and often contains a site map or list of links to the other pages on the site. From there other pages or sites can be navigated to by clicking on a link on the page already opened, by choosing a site from a list of 'favourites' or 'bookmarks' (which the user can add to in order to create a personal list) or by typing a site address in the box towards the top of the browser.

These addresses are properly known as URLs (Uniform Resource Locators, like http://www.bbc.co.uk – although most URLs begin with 'www' to show they're websites, this isn't actually necessary, as in http://news.bbc.co.uk). You may well be able to omit the 'http://' – most web browsers will add it automatically.

HTTP stands for Hypertext Transfer Protocol, the set of rules and standards that HTML/web pages adhere to and which govern the communications between an HTTP client (i.e. a web browser) and server (website). As mentioned above, this part of the URL can be changed to access non-web parts of the internet: 'telnet://' for example.

Many websites and services include pages of FAQs (frequently asked questions), which give a question-and-answer introduction to the site/service (though FAQs can be applied to any other topic for that matter). These can be very useful, and are often essential in the absence of any other form of documentation or guidance.

Web pages are multimedia-enabled so, as well as text, full-colour graphics and photographs, they can contain sound and moving images, including those from live webcams, though your PC has to have the right software to view or listen to these media. Often the required software can be downloaded from a website, and the site you're accessing may offer to download the required software straight away. You have to beware of viruses whenever downloading is involved, so ideally your PC should have a virus-checker installed. If it's attached to a network, it's possible that you won't have the requisite permissions to install such extras (often called 'plug-ins'); speak to your IT department about this.

Security again is paramount nowadays, as the web vies with e-mail as the method of choice for spreading viruses. In addition, there are other dangers on the web: innocently clicking on a link can start a download of malware onto your machine. There are many different types of malware besides the virus: adware and spyware might be downloaded, the latter leading to the possibility of identity theft; auto-diallers can be surreptitiously downloaded and secretly replace the original dialler, leading to huge phone bills; and 'phishing' can also be used to steal personal details. This latter practice involves a convincing-looking copy of a legitimate site where sensitive information like credit card numbers is entered.

As well as visiting other people's websites, it is quite possible to create your own. Most ISPs offer storage space for just such a 'web presence' as part of your subscription. As already mentioned, part of your organization's intranet can be made available to an international audience in the form of an extranet. The creation of a website as the widely available face of the library has become the norm, though library pages will probably be part of a larger site where the library is part of a larger organization. Links to many of these, all over the world, can be found at www.libdex.com.

The latest web feature to be used by libraries is the 'blog' or weblog – a sort of online diary of news, events and opinions, regularly updated; there can also be a searchable archive of past entries and facilities for readers to add their own comments. They can be used by libraries to publicise new developments, for updating and as a pointer to resources. The best known UK example is probably Gateshead Libraries' Et Cetera at www.libraryweblog.com; links can be found at libdex again: www.libdex.com/weblogs.html.

RSS should also be mentioned here (said to stand for various things, including really simple syndication and rich site summary). Also known as newsfeeds, this web-browser add-on informs you whenever a selected site or list of sites has changed, for example news headlines or additions to blogs or directories. Although useful for continual updating, there is the danger of selecting too many sites and being overwhelmed by information overload.

Search engines

If you don't have a specific URL to type in, you'll need to search for the information you require using a search engine. The home page of a typical search engine contains a space for you to type in a word or words that describe the subject: the engine searches its index for the text you've entered and returns a list of websites that contain that word or words, together with a link to each website listed. If you enclose the words in double quotes the search is for that particular phrase, otherwise the words can appear anywhere in the document; engines vary as to whether (and if so how) they apply the Boolean terms 'and', 'or' and 'not': there is usually a link to advanced search options that explain this and other options, such as how to narrow or broaden the search.

There are several types of search engine:

- general engines that index a large part of the web and can return many pages of 'hits' (as a general rule, unless you're getting desperate, just check the first 20 or so hits)
- directory engines
- specialized subject search engines
- natural language engines like Ask Jeeves

- website engines
- geographical engines (e.g. Google and Yahoo! allow you to specify UK sites only)
- multi-search tools which contain several different search engines at one site (you choose which to search from, the results from different engines being presented separately)
- meta-search tools which search several engines simultaneously, aiming to avoid site duplication in the resulting merged listing.

Many of the sites listed in the search results will in their turn have links to other sites, and so visiting any one site can turn into a browsing session from one site to the next, trying to find just the right information: this is web surfing, which can be great fun, but also a great time-waster.

There are hundreds of search engines, so only a few of the best-known and most popular ones are listed here:

Search engines
- alltheweb.com (search engine version of Yahoo!)
- goto.myway.com
- tinyurl.co.uk/bzy3 (for CompletePlanet, a Deep Web search engine)
- www.altavista.com (includes Babel Fish translator)
- www.ask.co.uk (Ask Jeeves)
- www.euroseek.com (Euro-centric)
- www.google.com
- www.information.com
- www.lycos.com
- www.teoma.com

Directories
- www.about.com (with named expert guides from over 20 countries)
- www.dmoz.org (biggest hand-built open directory on the net)
- www.galaxy.com
- www.go.com
- www.infospace.com
- www.looksmart.com
- www.ukplus.com (UK-centric)
- www.yahoo.com (probably the most popular directory on the web)

Multi/meta-search engines

- clusty.com
- www.allonesearch.com (access to over 500 search tools)
- www.dogpile.com
- www.info.com
- www.kartoo.com
- www.mamma.com (largest independent meta-search tool)
- www.metacrawler.com
- www.search.com
- www.surfwax.com

Yahoo! offers a hierarchically organized directory of subject categories as well as a standard search engine; the result of a query is a list of relevant categories, a list of sites and, at the bottom, a list of other search engines where the same query has been tried. This variety of approaches makes it a good engine to try first.

Google has been the most popular search engine for several years, to such an extent that the phrase 'to google' for something has entered the language as a synonym for web searching. This popularity was earned by its simplicity, uncluttered appearance, user-friendliness and intuitive feel, and the way it lists hits according to how many links there are to the sites listed, so that the most 'important' or relevant should be towards the top. However it has come under increasing criticism of late, particularly due to the 'most relevant' algorithm being skewed by blog results – many bloggers link to each other on a particular topic with the result that the top-listed results may not be the actual subject searched for, but blogs of people writing about it. The lesson here is that it is always a good idea not to rely on only one tool: try a variety of engines and directories.

Search engines sift through literally billions of pages of information but even so they're only partially covering total web content, even apart from the so-called 'Deep' or 'Invisible' web, consisting of searchable databases, the results from which can only be discovered by a direct query. There are estimated to be some 45 billion static web pages publicly available, but more than 200 billion database-driven pages available as dynamic database reports: Google indexes a little over eight billion pages (see netforbeginners.about.com/cs/secondaryweb1/a/secondaryweb.htm and www.brightplanet.com/deepcontent).

The disadvantage of all the general search engines is the vast amount of irrelevant, trivial, misleading stuff they retrieve, but this is an inescapable concomitant of the freedom of the web. The problem is trying to find as much as possible of the really high-quality, relevant content on the web that is often in danger of being swamped by the rubbish. A related danger is that many users have an uncritical faith in the quality of web sources, emphasizing the need for user education in the area of quality guidance.

So, rather than a general search engine, a subject gateway may be more useful. These provide searchable and browsable catalogues of websites, based on subject areas and selected according to quality criteria. Many subject gateways can be found through the Internet Public Library and Pinakes (which contains links to about 50 gateways). The Resource Discovery Network (RDN), aimed at the UK FE and HE communities, provides access to a number of faculty-level hubs, each a service in its own right containing a number of related subject gateways. Cross-searching is an important feature of RDN: you can search across an individual gateway, across all the gateways in a hub or across the whole of RDN.

Advantages of the web

The web provides:

- access to masses of information
- information that is mostly free or low-cost
- international coverage
- commercial sources
- access via a single port of call to online sources not originally part of the net/web
- a common interface and search strategies
- user-friendly, intuitive interfaces
- a popular, modish medium
- access from just about anywhere.

Disadvantages of the web

On the other hand, the web has:

- the bandwidth problem (slow connections, at least for dial-up)
- unreliable telecomm links
- the quantity-over-quality approach
- search engines/strategies not tailored to data
- the indiscriminate association of 'value' with any electronic source

- potential for time-wasting
- misleading, even false, information
- possibly offensive material
- material that may be out of date, undated, mis-dated or obsolete.

Appendix: UK government initiatives

Politicians have come to accept the potential of IT and especially the internet for enhancing education, lifelong learning and the economy, and for meeting people's information, cultural and recreational needs. In the UK this has been officially recognized by the government in the form of a number of web-based IT initiatives, many of which have had and will continue to have a big effect on libraries.

The People's Network

Launched in 2002 and funded by the New Opportunities Fund (NOF – now the Big Lottery Fund), this project sought to connect all public libraries UK-wide to the internet by 2005. The sum of £100 million was provided for equipment and connectivity, and another £20 million for IT training for public library staff. By the end of 2004 more than 30,000 computers with broadband internet access and a suite of basic applications had been installed in more than 4000 libraries across the UK, and about 40,000 library staff had received IT training.

The *UK Online Report* for 2003 stated that 10% of all UK internet users had used a public library to access the internet recently, while a recent MORI survey found that 16% of the public aged 16 and over had accessed the internet from a public library. Indeed, so great has been the success of this project that demand has led to the rationing of resources by way of advance booking and time limits on use (Halper, 2004; Hardie-Boys, 2004; Framework for the Future, 2003).

Incidentally, NOF also provided £230 million for ICT training for teachers and school librarians.

Framework for the Future

This is the name of the government's ten-year vision for public libraries, published by the Department for Culture, Media and Sport in 2003 and available from www.mla.gov.uk/information/publications/00pubs.asp.

One of the four strands of this vision comprises digital citizenship, aiming to build on the success of the People's Network and develop it from a project to a permanent service giving access to resources, to enable libraries to play a part in achieving e-government (UK Online) targets, to improve access to library stock by networking library catalogues, and to help overcome the digital and social exclusion that prevents people with special needs and others from accessing online resources.

At the time of writing the most advanced development is the building of a web-based access point for these services: an online enquiry service is already piloting (at www.peoplesnetwork.gov.uk/services/chat_form.html) prior to full roll-out later in 2005, with community information services and a 'virtual reference shelf' to follow.

UK Online and Learndirect

These are both administered by Ufi Ltd (the University for Industry). The UK Online network of centres was set up in 2000 to introduce people to the internet and teach basic IT skills in support of the government's commitment to make all government services available electronically by the end of 2005. Public libraries are just one of the types of venue in which a UK Online centre might be found (other places are internet cafés, colleges, community centres and village halls).

There are some 6000 across the country attracting about 50,000 users per week (www.egovmonitor.com/node/375), and they are seen as a vital access point for the socially excluded and for those living in deprived areas, especially for e-government services (Cabinet Office & DTI, 2005).

Learndirect centres provide access to computers from which to access online courses: there are some 2000 centres in the UK found in public libraries and places such as sports clubs, leisure and community centres, churches, university campuses and even railway stations. The specially-created courses cover computers, office skills, business and management, languages and self-development (see www.learndirect.co.uk).

Some useful URLs
Government sites
www.culture.gov.uk (Department for Culture, Media and Sport)
www.direct.gov.uk (Citizen Portal: single point of entry to government information services)
www.mla.gov.uk (Museums, Libraries and Archives Council)

www.mla.gov.uk/action/framework/framework.asp (Framework for the
  Future website)
www.ngfl.gov.uk (National Grid for Learning)
www.peoplesnetwork.gov.uk (People's Network Service)
www.ufi.com/ukol (UK Online centres)

Library sites

catalogue.bl.uk (BL catalogue)
www.ariadne.ac.uk/issue40/public-libraries/ (article on library weblogs)
www.ask-a-librarian.org.uk (ask a librarian)
www.bl.uk (British Library)
www.freepint.com/issues/090103.htm (scroll down for article on digital
  libraries – many links)
www.libdex.com (links to 18,000 library websites – global)
www.libdex.com/weblogs.html (links to library weblogs)
www.libraryweblog.com (Gateshead Libraries' weblog)

Online digital collections

eserver.org (35,000 free articles and texts in the arts and humanities)
onlinebooks.library.upenn.edu (index – listing over 20,000 free books on
  the web)
print.google.com/googleprint/library.html (digitizing contents of several
  major research libraries)
www.archive.org/details/millionbooks (planning to digitize a million free-
  to-read books)
www.bibliomania.org (free online literature with more than 2000 classic
  texts)
www.digitalbookindex.org (index – links to more than 100,000 records
  from more than 1800 sites)
www.gutenberg.org (15,000 freely downloadable out-of-copyright texts)

IT sites

lii.org (Librarians' Index to the Internet)
netforbeginners.about.com (tutorials and information about the internet
  and web)
www.about.com/compute (introductions/guides for beginners)
www.librarytechnology.org (information on library automation)

www.multimedia-world.co.uk (CD-ROM catalogue)

www.pctechguide.com (guide to PC technology – internals and peripherals)

www.whatis.com (IT encyclopedia – terminology explained)

Open Source software

dewey.library.nd.edu/mylibrary (for building a portal – an interface to web resources)

library.rider.edu/scholarly/ecorrado/il2004/ossfeatures.html (ILS comparisons and links)

www.dspace.org (digital archiving system)

www.fsf.org (Free Software Foundation – 'free as in free speech, not free beer')

www.greenstone.org/cgi-bin/library (software for building/distributing digital library collections)

www.koha.org (best-known open source ILS)

www.opensource.org (Open Source Initiative)

www.oss4lib.org (OSS for libraries)

www.oss4lib.org/readings/oss4lib-getting-started.php (integrated library systems – 1999)

www.vuw.ac.nz/staff/brenda_chawner/biblio.html (bibliography on OSS and libraries)

Virtual/hybrid libraries

hylife.unn.ac.uk/toolkit/ (brief report on the hybrid library concept – last updated 2001)

www.bubl.ac.uk (subject gateway)

www.hw.ac.uk/libwww/irn/pinakes/pinakes.html (subject gateways)

www.infotoday.com/online/ol2000/pack9.html (report on Compaq's WebLibrary)

www.ipl.org (Internet Public Library – 'providing library resources to internet users')

www.rdn.ac.uk/ (Resource Discovery Network)

www.vlib.org.uk (example of a virtual library)

www.vts.rdn.ac.uk/ (Virtual Training Suite – online tutorials for IT and internet skills)

Community information

www.thisisbath.com and www.bath.co.uk (two examples of community
    information on the web)

General sites

dir.yahoo.com/news_and_media (links to newspaper and broadcasting
    websites)
en.wikipedia.org (online encyclopaedia)
news.bbc.co.uk (BBC news site)
www.bbc.co.uk (BBC's general site)
www.britannica.com (Encyclopaedia Britannica online)
www.thepaperboy.com.au (links to newspaper websites, with separate
    UK section)
w.moreover.com (Anglo-US news sources – over 1600 covered – seven-
    day free trial)

Directory information

www.yell.co.uk (Yellow Pages)
www.scoot.co.uk (Yellow Pages rival, part of BT Directories)
www2.bt.com/edq_resnamesearch (directory enquiries)

Further reading

Buckley, P. and Clark, D. (2004) *The Rough Guide to the Internet 2005*,
    London, Rough Guides.

References

Cabinet Office and DTI (2005) Cabinet Office: Prime Minister's Strategy
    Unit, *Connecting the UK: the digital strategy*, London, Cabinet Office,
    joint report with Department of Trade and Industry,
    www.strategy.gov.uk/work_areas/digital_strategy/report/index.asp.
Framework for the Future (2003) Department for Culture, Media and
    Sport, *Framework for the Future: libraries, learning and information
    in the next decade*, London, DCMS,
    www.culture.gov.uk/global/publications/archive_2003/framework_
    future.htm.
Halper, S. (2004) Evaluating the Impact of the People's Network,

Library and Information Update, **3** (12), December, 34–5.

Hardie-Boys, N. (2004) *The People's Network: evaluation summary*, (Big Lottery Fund Research, Issue 7, November 2004), London, Big Lottery Fund. www.mla.gov.uk/information/publications/00pubs.asp.

7 The management perspective

Jane Gill

This is a revision of a chapter written in the previous edition by Lyn Pullen.

Libraries do not function within a vacuum, but are there to serve either the general public or the clientèle of the particular institution concerned. This chapter looks at the wider context within which libraries function and the trends and initiatives currently affecting them.

The role of libraries in the UK

Academic and workplace libraries have a clear role in serving the needs of their institution: a college library has to support the curricula offered, a hospital library supplies the needs of the doctors and other staff and a firm's library concentrates on topics relevant to its particular business. Public libraries, however, fulfil multiple roles, and the emphasis placed on each role tends to vary over time according to the aims of the particular local authority served. It is both a major strength and a weakness that public libraries try to be all things to all people – a strength in that they are potentially of relevance to the entire population, and a weakness in that there are insufficient resources to achieve this end. The tendency is, therefore, to offer a limited service in all areas, which satisfies nobody entirely. There is a need to identify the roles of the service, to be clear as to their order of priority and to target the sectors of the community that are to be the main focus of the service at any given time.

The UK's public library service came into being in the 19th century to be the 'poor man's university'. As such it fulfilled a primarily educational role, but over the years roles concerning information and leisure have also developed; these three roles can be most easily remembered in the phrase 'education, information and recreation'. There has always been a community role too: public libraries are unique in offering much of their service free at the point of use, in serving anybody who walks through the door, without question or prejudice, and for being safe places where even the more vulnerable members of society feel free to visit and meet. The late 20th century saw the addition of IT which, although it is only a tool for achieving the first three roles mentioned above, is using up such a significant proportion of the resources available that it is worth considering as a role in its own right.

The government is currently emphasizing education in all its aspects, and includes in this the need for the UK to have an IT-literate population, seeing the ability to grasp the advantages of IT as key to the future economic prosperity of the country. Libraries are seen as places which provide ICT and staff help to their users. The provision of this service has multiple aims:

- to allow free access to computers and the internet for everybody, so that a divide does not build up between those who do and those who do not possess computers
- to assist people in developing their ICT skills
- to give access to digital learning materials, which are set to increase in both quality and quantity
- to provide staff expertise to seek out information or learning materials – staff become skilled gatekeepers not just of printed sources but of the digitized ones too
- to provide greater and easier access to public services – the government has set a target date of 2005 for government services (national and local) to be online (referred to as 'e-government').

The leisure role of libraries – usually equated with the lending of books and other items – is tending to receive less attention from central government, though there is an expectation that it will be maintained. It is also seen as a core function by many of its users. Library staff have a proactive role in this area in helping to inculcate the reading habit early in life and in helping people enrich their reading experience, through guidance and promotion (see the reading development section later in this chapter).

Government policies are having an effect on which of their roles public libraries are emphasizing, because much funding now comes directly from central government in the form of funds for specific purposes, which have to be competed for.

The future role of libraries is discussed at the end of this chapter.

Social inclusion

Another very strong theme of central government is social inclusion. The UK government's Social Exclusion Unit defines social exclusion as 'a shorthand term for what can happen when people or areas suffer from a combination of linked problems such as unemployment, poor skills, low incomes, poor housing, high crime environments, bad health and family breakdown' (www.socialexclusion.gov.uk). Socially excluded groups therefore include:

- unemployed people
- homeless people
- people of low educational achievement (including people who are illiterate)
- people with few skills to offer in the workplace
- people on low incomes
- people suffering ill health
- minority groups, such as travellers or ethnic groups
- people with limited mobility, whether through disability, poverty or through being carers who are unable to leave those for whom they care.

As individuals, people may become excluded because they suffer from isolation, lack of identity, low self-confidence, low self-esteem, dependence, fear, anger, low aspirations or hopelessness.

Combating social exclusion means reducing disparity (of income, of educational achievement), discrimination and disadvantage, while encouraging recognition of the value of diversity.

Libraries have a lot to offer the social inclusion agenda. They are open to everybody, free at the point of use, treat everybody equally, are non-judgemental and have caring, helpful staff. They offer educational opportunities directly through their bookstock and their computers and indirectly via their ability to refer people on to other institutions. They offer information, which is the keystone of a democratic society and essential to individuals in their own lives, and they offer a means of developing the individual's imagination, awareness and creativity.

Libraries do, however, have to examine themselves to ensure they really are the all-welcoming, all-inclusive institutions they believe themselves to be. In reality many library services are predominantly middle-class institutions, staffed by and used by people of a particular class, age range and ethnic and social background. The Department for Culture, Media and Sport (DCMS, 2001) is expecting all library services to put together a social inclusion strategy that makes social inclusion a priority within the service and looks at areas such as:

- what specific services need to be tailored to meet the needs of minority groups and communities
- consulting and involving socially excluded groups
- tailoring opening hours and the location of service points to reflect the needs of the community
- developing the role of libraries as community resource centres, providing access to communication as well as information
- libraries being a major vehicle for providing free access to ICT at local level
- libraries becoming the 'local learning place' and the champion of the independent learner, and forming partnerships with other learning organizations.

The last point on this list emphasizes one key point in combating social exclusion: no single agency can achieve it in isolation. It is the remit of the government's Social Exclusion Unit to bring together various areas of national and local government and enable the creation of 'joined-up solutions to joined-up problems'. Libraries need to heed this, and to make strong efforts to work in partnership with other local government departments, especially those concerned with education, and with other agencies and the voluntary sector.

Business planning

Management in UK libraries has changed significantly over the last 20 years. Today it is expected that public and large academic libraries will regularly measure various aspects of their service, will know who uses their service and why, and will enter into two-way communication with their users. Academic libraries have to do this within the context of their institution, and public libraries within the parameters set by their authority and those set by central government.

There are many ways of formulating a business plan, but the basic idea of all of them is to:

- monitor the business, i.e. measure how it is doing; for libraries this might include:
  — how much the service is costing per person served
  — how many people are using it, and whether they are satisfied with it
  — how many people are not using it and why not
  — how many items are being issued annually
  — how high the staff turnover is
- review the business, using the monitoring data collected, and asking such questions as:
  — what does it exist to do and is this still valid and viable?
  — how does it do it?
  — how successfully does it do it?
  — what do its customers think of it?
- plan changes to the business, which might include:
  — changing what the business does; in public libraries, this might mean a change of emphasis, such as lessening the provision of leisure reading and increasing the educational role
  — changing the services offered; introducing new audiovisual or IT services, for example
  — looking for efficiency savings or ways of bringing in more income to provide the budget for extending services
- implement the changes.

The cycle then starts again, with the changed service being monitored and reviewed, then further changes planned and implemented. In practice this cycle is going on all the time at all levels, from the strategic to the day-to-day routines, but most services consciously apply the cycle on a yearly basis and create some sort of annual business plan to record the process.

Public libraries and UKcentral government
Framework for the Future: libraries, learning and information in the next decade

Launched in February 2003, Framework for the Future is the government's first ever national public library strategy, setting out a long-term vision for the public library service in England (Framework for the Future, 2003). The strategy puts forward a programme for transforming existing strengths into a service that is designed to meet the needs of the 21st century . The public library service with its long history of serving the community is seen as being ideally placed to assist local councils plan their services to meet the needs of local citizens.

The central themes of Framework for the Future are:

- books, reading and learning
- digital citizenship
- community and civic values.

Libraries have a central role to play in delivering the shared priorities of central and local government:

- in education for children, adults and families
- in building stronger, more sustainable and safer communities
- in improving the quality of life of older people and people at risk
- in communicating messages across the whole range of public services and meeting information needs.

The Museums Libraries and Archives Council (MLA), which was launched in April 2000 and replaced the Museums and Galleries Commission (MGC) and the Library and Information Commission (LIC), was commissioned by the DCMS to develop a three-year action plan to develop the main themes identified in Framework for the Future (www.mla.gov.uk).

National standards for UK public libraries

In 1998 the government introduced a series of developments to establish national standards for public libraries (www.culture.gov.uk/global/ publications/archive_2004/library_standards.htm).

From 1998, all 149 English public library authorities were required to submit an Annual Library Plan to the Secretary of State for Culture Media and Sport which both reviewed past performance and set out strategies for the coming year.

Three years later, in 2001, a set of 26 public library standards was introduced by the DCMS in order to set out what was meant by a 'comprehensive and efficient service'. These were seen as complementary to Annual Library Plans.

Towards the end of 2002 Annual Library Plans were replaced by Public Library Position statements. These position statements had to be submitted for a maximum of two years by all library authorities except those which received an 'Excellent' overall Comprehensive Performance Assessment or a 'Good' overall assessment with an 'Excellent' Libraries and Leisure score. Position statements were intended to show how public library authorities planned to deliver their services in line with the main themes within Framework for the Future and to give an indication of their current service levels. Any improvements to the service were to be included with supporting evidence of policies and practices.

In 2004 the 26 national standards were reduced to a set of ten, the Public Library Service Standards. Designed to show how libraries are meeting the needs of their local community, they are:

- PLSS 1 – proportion of households living within specified distance of a static library.
- PLSS 2 – aggregate scheduled opening hours per 1000 population for all libraries
- PLSS 3 – percentage of static libraries as defined by CIPFA (The Chartered Institute of Public Finance and Accountancy) providing access to electronic information resources connected to the internet
- PLSS 4 – total number of electronic workstations with access to the internet and the library's catalogue available to users per 10,000 population
- PLSS 5 – requests
  — percentage of requests for books met within seven days
  — percentage of requests for books met within 15 days
  — percentage of requests for books met within 30 days
- PLSS 6 – number of library visits per 1000 population
- PLSS 7 – percentage of library users 16 and over who view their library service as
  — very good
  — good
  — adequate
  — poor
  — very poor
- PLSS 8 – percentage of library users under 16 who view their library service as
  — good
  — adequate
  — bad
- PLSS 9 – annual items added through purchase per 1000 population

- PLSS 10 – time taken to replenish the lending stock on open access or available on loan.

The service standards will be complemented by a second element: 'impact measures'. The first set of public library impact measures, developed in the context of Framework for the Future, was launched in March 2005. They were selected to show evidence of public libraries' value to and impact on people and communities. They show the contribution libraries make to the following five shared priorities agreed by central and local government:

- raising standards across schools
- improving the quality of life for children, young people, families at risk and older people
- promoting healthier communities
- creating safer and stronger communities
- promoting the economic vitality of communities.

Academic libraries

There is no set format for academic libraries to follow, although most university or college libraries will have some sort of annual plan, which will be part of their institution's wider plan. There are some guidelines published to assist the process. The CILIP Colleges of Further and Higher Education Group (CoFHE) issues *Guidelines for Colleges: recommendations for learning resources* (Eynon, 2005), which is updated regularly, and the Council for Learning Resources in Colleges (CoLRiC) offers free of charge their *Guidelines for Self-assessment of College Learning Resources Services* (CoLRiC, n.d.), which is used by their own inspectors.

Finding out what users want
Why do we need to know?

No business will survive if it does not provide what its users want, though for libraries this is complicated by other stakeholders controlling the service to some extent. Public libraries are accountable not only to the public directly, but also to the local councillors, who represent the public, and to national government and other funders, while academic and workplace libraries are also responsible to their institutions or firms. All libraries must still regularly explore what is wanted of them, not only by the people who use them, but also by those who do not use them, so they can consider changing their service to attract these non-users.

Methods of finding out

There are many ways of finding out what people think of the library service; which method is used depends on what information is wanted and the resources available to undertake the research. Possible methods include:

* comment forms or questionnaires, asking users or non-users to write what they think about aspects of the service
* staff feedback – the front-line staff will know a lot about what the users think of the service and can usefully feed this information into the planning process
* mystery shopping – this might test an enquiry service by a person being sent in to ask a set of specific questions and reporting back on how well the questions were answered, how polite the staff were, etc.
* meetings with the user or non-user – these can take many forms, and may be meetings with individual users or with groups of users; some control over the topics covered is usually advisable to ensure that sufficient focus is achieved to produce a useful outcome and to help prevent opinionated individuals skewing the results
* presentations or exhibitions – which can serve the dual purpose of informing people about the service and seeking their views on it.

Public libraries in the UK can now use a nationally available public survey system called PLUS (Public Library User Survey) to find out what their users think of their service; there is a standardized questionnaire and the results can be analysed (for a fee). Some of the questions involved try to measure quality as well as quantity, covering topics such as the helpfulness of the staff, the quality of the stock and the layout of the building. Some of the information derived from the survey, along with other statistics, has to be reported each year to CIPFA, and the results from all the authorities are published to enable comparisons.

It is important that the consultation process is not one-way: if at all possible, feedback should be given to those giving their opinions on what, if anything, will be done about the points raised. It is important that people know they are being listened to and the reasons behind decisions taken.

There is an excellent document called *How to Consult your Users*, available on the Cabinet Office's website at www.cabinet-office.gov.uk/.

Non-users

Academic libraries have something of a captive audience, and students may well find their course necessitates using the library. Public libraries, however, are open to people to use or not as they choose, and although most people think public libraries are a good idea, not all use them, and this must be an area of concern. Obviously, not everyone will choose to use their library, but it is important to know the reason for this choice, and if the reason is something that the library service can influence, to encourage greater use.

Non-users are a lot more difficult to survey than users, but one accessible group is lapsed users. Authorities who have carried out lapsed user surveys find that the major reasons for people who have used libraries to stop doing so (other than personal reasons) are that they find the opening hours of the library inconvenient or the range of stock insufficient. People who have never used a library are often ignorant of what the service has to offer them, or are under the impression that there is a charge involved, so there is obviously much that can be done to increase awareness of the service, but it is also necessary to look at the services offered and the image of the service to achieve a socially inclusive service, as discussed above.

Measuring the service

The different aspects of library services vary in terms of how easy they are to measure. It is easy to measure quantitative things, such as how many books were issued last year. It is less easy to assess how an activity such as issuing books contributed qualitatively to the life of the person who borrowed the book. Did it fire their imagination to write their own book or visit a foreign country? Did it give them the information they needed to start their own business? Did it help them pass an exam so they could get a better job? And what effect did this change to the individual have on society? We must have ways of judging how well our service is doing, but we must take care that we don't just measure those things that are easily measurable.

One of the dangers in this area is for the public services to try and use measuring techniques from the commercial sector without considering the different nature of their 'business'. The commercial sector is interested in selling its services to those who can afford to buy them: the big bookshop chains, for example, are aiming at the professional classes, who are more likely to come from a book-orientated background and have the money to buy books. Public libraries are very different in that they exist to serve everyone and to give any individual a fair share of this community resource, though increasingly they are prioritizing services to those who have no other access to books and information.

The way in which a service is measured affects the service itself: if you judge the success of a library on the number of books it issues, then you only have to concentrate on buying popular fiction to be successful; if you believe that quality literature is also important, you have to treat issue figures as only one measure, and find other ways for measuring the impact of the less frequently issued areas of stock.

Measures, often called performance indicators or PIs, are collected by all libraries. Some of these may be required by the institution that the library serves, or by outside bodies, but many are collected by choice as a way of seeing how well the service is doing and judging how to allocate the budget. This exercise is taken one step further by the setting of targets. A public library may determine that 45% of the people in its catchment area are registered as users, and may set itself the target of increasing this to 50% over a three-year period. Targets help to focus activity and it is more motivating for all the staff involved to concentrate on specific areas for a time, to see a real improvement achieved and then to move on to other areas; the alternative is to try and do a little of everything all the time, but this spreads effort so thinly that no measurable progress can be identified.

The standards are likely to be good for library services. The targets set can be used to justify adequate funding: public libraries have been repeatedly squeezed over the years of cuts to local government budgets, and the setting of standards will hopefully show that there is a level below which it is not acceptable to fall and that central government takes libraries seriously enough to be willing to enforce the standards. The problem is that they are standards set by central government for a service funded by local government, and no funds are being offered to help meet them; more money for libraries probably means cuts to services elsewhere, and each local authority will view the matter differently.

Inspection of academic libraries in the UK

College and university libraries are inspected as part of their institutions on a regular basis. Higher education establishments have to answer to the Higher Education Funding Council (HEFC), and further education establishments to the new Learning and Skills Councils (LSC). These are the bodies that fund universities and colleges, so the inspections are of great importance. The library tends to be inspected every time: in higher education the inspections are carried out on a subject basis, so it is likely the library will be examined for its support of the area being covered, and in further education the entire college is inspected every time.

The actual inspection is carried out in the higher education sector on a six-yearly basis, by a body called the Quality Assurance Agency, which is an independent body set up in 1997 to provide an integrated quality assurance service for universities. In further education the FEFC (Further Education Funding Council) has always done the inspections, on a four-yearly basis, and this function now passes to the LSC. The approach is one of self-assessment, with the institution grading itself and the inspectors checking the grades. As the inspection covers the whole institution, the areas looked at are ones like 'curriculum design, content and organization', 'teaching, learning and assessment' and 'student progression and attainment'; libraries will be covered under 'learning resources'. Libraries may find that they are not given very much attention in the inspection: the inspection team does not usually include any librarians, and the library is not looked at separately but as part of a larger area. In further education, libraries are regarded as part of 'central services' along with buildings and computers. This may not be helpful to the library in arguing for improved funding for its services from its institution's budget.

Benchmarking

One way of measuring performance is to see how you have done this year compared with last year, or with five years ago. Another is to compare yourself with other libraries or library services similar to your own. This is not generally done by academic libraries, who tend to be answerable only to their own institution, but is increasingly undertaken by public libraries, who are compared with other public library services both by government and by the people who use them.

Many statistics on public libraries are collected and published each year by CIPFA, so it is possible to see how various services are performing as measured by these statistics. The work of doing the comparisons is complex and onerous, however, so it is now possible to join a benchmarking club. This means a library service pays for its data to be compared with that of other library services and allows those other services to see its data.

This is very useful information but, as always with statistics, the end result must be treated with caution. It is difficult to ensure that everyone is answering the same question in the same way (especially where budgets are concerned) and that you are measuring like with like: to see a figure for salaries in a London borough and compare it with salaries elsewhere, you have to take into account that the cost of living in London tends to be higher than elsewhere. To help ensure that any given area is measured against others that are comparable, authorities belong to 'family groups' for statistical purposes, with each member of a group having been assessed by the statisticians to ensure demographic likeness. Factors that are taken into account include how many elderly people live in the area and how many extra people come into the area to work (and therefore use the local services) each day.

Best value

The Labour government which came to power in the UK in 1997 expressed its determination to see the process of government modernized (the key document is the 1999 White Paper *Modernizing Local Government* (DETR, 1998)). All local authorities are therefore now under a legal obligation continuously to improve the economy, efficiency and effectiveness of all their activities and functions, though it is emphasized that best value is about the quality of services, not just about doing everything as cheaply as possible.

The Local Government Act 1999 provides powers for the government to specify standards of performance that must be met. Failure to meet a performance standard will normally be judged as a failure to achieve best value for that particular service.

Best value performance indicators

The government sets some performance indicators which local authorities must report on, and expects each authority to add its own. As of 2004/2005, the government indicators that specifically applied to public libraries were:

• the cost per physical visit to public libraries

- the number of physical visits per 1000 population to public library premises
- the percentage of library users who found the book/information they wanted, or reserved it, and were satisfied with the outcome
- the percentage of residents satisfied with local authority cultural services.

Each year, authorities must publish their results for each indicator, and set targets to be reached for the following three years; if targets are not met, explanations must be made.

Best value performance indicators (BVPIs) are reviewed regularly and in June 2004 the Office of the Deputy Prime Minister published a consultation document setting out the government's proposals for changes to the BVPIs for the financial year 2005/2006. See the Office of the Deputy Prime Minister's local government performance site for key facts and up-to-date information about best value and performance indicators: www.bvpi.gov.uk.

Comprehensive Performance Assessment

Comprehensive Performance Assessment (CPA) was introduced by the government in December 2002. It measures how well councils are delivering services for local people and communities. External inspectors from the Audit Commission not only look at documents produced, but will also visit the authority to seek any further information they think necessary and carry out reality checks, looking at the service for themselves and talking to users and staff. At the end, the authority will receive a score that reflects how well services are being delivered and whether there are indications for improvement where a low score is returned.

Finance and resources

A library receives a certain amount of money for running its service from its institution, business or council, as explained in Chapter 1. Years ago, this was the end of the story, but nowadays public and academic libraries are expected to find sources of income from elsewhere as well.

Income generation

Income generation is about making charges – usually small – for parts of the service. Common examples are:

- charges for overdue items
- reservation fees
- hire fees for audiovisual materials
- charges for room hire
- charges for photocopying or printouts from computers.

The core service in public libraries – usually defined as the lending of books and the provision of information – has to be free by law, but the local authority has the discretion to charge for other things, although the government is making it very clear that it does not wish there to be any charge for the provision of computers. Beyond this, each authority makes its own decisions, though in reality there is very little difference between what is charged for, or the level of fees set.

Since incorporation, universities and colleges have seen themselves as businesses rather than services, but this has not led to their libraries seeking to generate income. What has happened in these libraries over the last few years is that they have tightened up on who can access their resources. Members of the general public and even students from other institutions may not be given access, or at least may not be given free access. These libraries do aim to recover their costs on such things as photocopying and computer printouts.

There is often an uncomfortable relationship in public libraries between the concept of giving a service and the need to generate income, especially regarding the extent of resources given to each. The library exists to give the service, but if it does not generate income there is less money with which to provide the service, so the choice as to where to concentrate resources is very difficult.

There is also direct conflict regarding the making of a charge: the ideal situation from a service point of view, for example, is for no books to be returned late, so all stock is regularly available for other users. From an income generation point of view, however, the more overdue books the better, as this brings in more money, and overdue charges are usually a substantial part of a library's income. Similar problems apply to the provision of audiovisual materials: do you look upon DVD hire as a purely income-generating function and manage it accordingly, or is it a service that happens to make money?

Even if the service is designated as purely commercial, library staff do not always have the knowledge or experience to maximize income by managing the income-generating parts of the service appropriately: there is much that could be learned from the commercial sector. One important difference between local authorities and businesses has to be remembered, however: local authorities are not allowed to 'trade', only to sell 'excess capacity'. This is a rule designed to protect traders from what could be seen as unfair competition such as if a library service were able to hire out videos more cheaply than the local video hire shop because the staff time used was paid for out of the public money provided for running the library. Whether libraries stay within the strictest definition of the law is something that has not yet been tested, which would only happen if a commercial enterprise brought a court case against a local authority.

Seeking outside funding

The other way of obtaining more money for the service is to make bids to funding bodies or seek sponsorship.

A lot of money is currently available from funding bodies. The government is making much use of this method of financing in order to steer spending to the areas it favours. The major sources at the moment are:

1 The lottery: The lottery funds that most often benefit libraries are the Big Lottery Fund and the Heritage Lottery fund. An example of the latter is a grant of nearly £1 million to Sevenoaks library, museum and art gallery for a project that is the first of its type in the country. The Kaleidoscope Project will revamp the library, adding a new café and extension while the art gallery will be enlarged and the museum modernized.
2 European funds: various.
3 ERASMUS: this is a European fund used extensively by colleges and universities. It is part of the European SOCRATES programme, which exists to promote lifelong learning and encourage access to education for all. ERASMUS is aimed specifically at higher education.

The provision of this money is obviously beneficial, but the need to seek funding in this way can cause problems. Each fund lays down very strict criteria as to what the money sought can be spent on, and it can be difficult to reconcile the money available with the long-term strategic aims and business plan of the library. The work involved in writing the bids for this sort of money is also very onerous, and often has to be carried out at short notice to very tight timescales.

Colleges and universities as institutions put a lot of time into bidding for funding, but this is not usually specific to their libraries. Again, the influence of the funding process can be seen in that they may be able to bid, for example, for money for 'isolated women returners', which may influence them (as is intended) to provide courses for this specific group of people.

Sponsorship, on the other hand, occurs when a body, usually a business, is asked to give the library money, goods in kind or staff help, in return for which they will receive some benefit – usually their name published somewhere so they receive advertising and, by association, validation from the library. An example is a firm sponsoring a library leaflet and receiving an acknowledgement and the inclusion of their logo in it. Libraries have a large clientèle, and are very well regarded, even by those who do not use them, so they can be very good places for sponsors to place their message. When approaching firms for sponsorship it is important to be clear what benefits are offered to the sponsor as well as what is wanted by the library.

What is the money spent on?

More and more is being expected of all sorts of libraries, as new formats and demands come into being (such as computers) while the existing ones rarely cease to exist, so that the money received has to be stretched further and further. The areas on which library money is spent are:

* staff
* buildings
* equipment
* materials (including the stock)
* supplies and services
* establishment costs.

What exactly is covered under these headings will vary with the type of library.

Staff: these costs account for 50% or more of the budget of most libraries. Salaries are the most obvious cost, but there are also additional costs to the employer for every member of staff, such as national insurance and pension contributions, as well as associated costs like training and travel.

Buildings: these costs may include vehicles, and will cover the running costs like heating, lighting, insurance, rubbish clearance and grounds maintenance. The value of the services' buildings may also have to be taken into account.

Equipment: this covers computer hardware and software, phones, faxes, security systems and funds for buying new furniture. Rather than outright purchase a lot of items are now leased over something like a three-year period.

Materials: by far the largest item in this category is likely to be the stock fund, which will probably also cover subscriptions to online services. Other items may include stationery (including readers' tickets, date labels, etc.) and publicity and cleaning materials.

Supplies and services: the major item here is likely to be licence and maintenance contracts on ICT hardware and software (e.g. the charge from the supplier for the use of the library circulation system).

Establishment costs: there are many services that a library needs to obtain, either externally or from its institution, and even if the service is internal, payment will probably be necessary. This will cover areas like personnel, legal and financial advice and help, as well as services such as payroll.

Income: this is usually another section on the budget sheet, showing what money has been received into the service. Some sort of trading account may have been set up, showing not only the income but also the money spent in order to generate the income – the purchase of the videos that are hired out, the publicity costs, etc. However the figures are shown, income-generating services should always be looked at in relation to the money they cost to run, and a decision is needed as to whether the staff time spent is taken into account, or if this cost is absorbed by the service generally.

How the money is spent

Local government budgets usually work on an annual cycle, and each authority will have its own rules regarding overspending or underspending the budget at the end of each year. A degree of over- or underspend may be 'rolled over' and set against the following year's budget. Significant overspends are a serious matter, and sufficient budgetary control should be maintained to avoid them, or at the very least flag them up in advance. Underspending carries the danger of the money remaining being taken away, and possibly even future budgets being reduced on the grounds that this is evidence that the money is not needed.

How the library budget is split between the various demands on it is decided individually by each public library service, or by the academic/workplace library in question. In public library services, which may have anything between ten and 100 branches, the degree of devolved responsibility for spending varies considerably. Spending decisions on the service's infrastructure – its buildings and staff in particular – tend to remain centralized as it is seldom practical to approach this in any other way.

Decisions on stock purchase may vary, from each branch having its own stockfund to a completely centralized system where a few staff undertake all purchasing; often the system compromises between the two extremes in some way. It is important that a library service should be seen as a whole, so a good range of stock is purchased; it is not advisable to have a high degree of duplication between branches, as this must mean that other titles are being ignored. A centralized system helps avoid this. On the other hand, it is important to be aware of the needs of any given library's community and respond to it, which is where local knowledge is invaluable. A blend of the two, together with good statistical data, is the best solution.

The vast majority of a library service's budget is fixed rather than discretionary, at least in the short term. The amount that has to be budgeted for rates, electricity and maintenance agreements cannot be reduced significantly. The staff budget, which will be over half of the total, is similarly difficult to reduce quickly. Staff have contracts that guarantee them employment unless their job ceases to exist, and removing posts, particularly at assistant level, will probably lead to partial or total library closures and public outcry. If budget reductions have to be made, or money has to be found to start a new service, there are very few areas of the budget that can be used: reducing the training budget is a short-sighted measure, as is reducing publicity and so on. The stockfund can be vulnerable in this circumstance, as it is easy for those outside the library world to think that a small or short-term reduction will not matter. It is true that a one-year 'blip' will not have a huge effect, but continuously low stockfunds will gradually erode the stock, and it takes a lot of money and effort to build it back up again.

All the expenditure discussed above is classed as revenue expenditure: it is spent on running the service. The other type of expenditure often referred to is capital, which is one-off expenditure such as building a new library or installing a new computer system. While libraries will receive revenue automatically every year (even if the amount is somewhat variable and may have to be argued for), capital expenditure usually has to be requested from the authority or the institution, and the library will be up against other services for its share of the fund.

One significant development in capital expenditure is the development of the Private Finance Initiative (PFI). This is a scheme whereby the cost of a new building will be borne by the private sector, who then lease it back to the authority over a long period of time (often 30 years). The long-term wisdom of this in terms of the ultimate cost is open to debate, but it may be the only way for some large capital sums to be obtained.

Brighton and Hove's Jubilee Library, which opened in spring 2005, is part of a £50 million PFI regeneration scheme. As reported in *Library and Information Update*, January/February 2005 (Brighton's New Jubilee Library, 2005) the mixture of retail, leisure, hotel, office and residential facilities is cross-subsidizing the £14 million cost of the new building.

Promoting the service

Public libraries are one of the country's best-kept secrets. They provide an amazing range and quality of services, but relatively few members of the public – even people who use their local library – have a very good idea of the full range of what is available to them.

The reasons for this are mixed, lack of funds being one of the major factors: there is often insufficient money to run the service itself, so it is difficult to justify spending on promotion. There is also, however, a sad lack of seeing the need to promote: library staff tend to be very good with the public in one-to-one situations, but not at going out and selling the service. The predominantly female bias of the library world may have something to do with this. Many men seem to find it comes more naturally to sound knowledgeable and put a positive spin on things; it has been said that a woman needs to feel she knows 75% of what there is to know about a subject before she will talk in public about it, where a man only needs to feel he knows 25%.

The professionalism with which promotion is carried out is also very variable, and can only partly be excused by lack of resources. This is a skill, like any other, and it is wise to use professionals or to learn how to do it properly in-house. The advent of computers with graphics packages is a mixed blessing – the horrors that can be perpetrated by someone with no design flair when let loose are worrying, and controlling this sort of output is very difficult. We live in an intensely visual age, where the public are used to high-quality design, and the amateur look is not one a library should tolerate.

Academic and workplace libraries, although to an extent they have captive audiences, also have to promote themselves to ensure their clientèle know what they have to offer (in the case of academic libraries, learning to use the library is part of the student's education). If libraries are not valued by their users, their budgets may be at risk, and with the advent of the internet, many users may feel they can seek their information via this source with no library intervention necessary.

Definitions

It is worth sorting out a few definitions in this area, as various terms tend to be used very loosely and with consequent confusion. The definitions below are as used in the marketing profession, and lay people will tend to use them more interchangeably:

1 Marketing is to do with all activities which ensure that consumers consume. It includes looking at the customers' needs and desires, educating the consumer about the product or service, developing strategies to persuade the consumer to buy (i.e. advertising and selling) and using the information gained to decide on product lines, pricing and promotion.
2 Promotion, when the word is used in a general sense, is the encouragement of the use of a service or the sale of a product. More specifically, a 'sales promotion' could be a money-off offer on a product.
3 Advertising is the paid, public announcement of a persuasive message.
4 Publicity, when the word is used in a general sense, is to do with increasing public interest or awareness about something; in the marketing world it means promotion obtained free of charge for a product or service (e.g. an article in a newspaper).
5 Selling is a person-to-person activity, such as when a car salesman sells you a car.
6 Public relations is the activity of ensuring an institution has a favourable image with the public.
7 Market research is the study of possible buyers of products or users of a service. It is an area which calls for a high degree of knowledge about how to achieve the set objectives: the information it produces is only as good as the clarity of the objectives set for the exercise and the phrasing of the questions asked. The best-known examples are carried out by big firms such as MORI and are very expensive.
8 Outreach is a term sometimes used in the library world to mean the taking out of services or information beyond the library premises, but

can also mean the provision of a service to a group in society who might otherwise be neglected.

How to promote your service well

Library publicity, especially in the public library world, tends to fail because of two things: an attempt to advertise everything to everyone, and confusion about promoting as opposed to giving information. The following is not intended to be an exhaustive lesson in how to promote a service, but a selection of relevant points to bear in mind. There is a CILIP group which specializes in this topic: the Publicity and Public Relations Group, which has published some excellent concise and easy-to-read publications (not all of which are now in print, but are worth seeking out). It has a quarterly newsletter, *Public Eye*.

1 Are you selling the service or informing people about it? If the former, and assuming we are talking about written publicity, you need very little text, but must be very aware of the image you are creating with your words, your images and your layout.
2 Target your publicity to your subject and your audience. When the budget is tight, the tendency is to do a few leaflets which try to explain the whole service to any sort of user. This is actually a tremendous waste of money, because it tells a lot of people about a lot of things they have no interest in – if they can be bothered to read it in the first place.
3 Know your target audience. Companies in the commercial sector spend millions on finding out who their consumers are, what they want and are likely to want in the future. You do not have these sorts of resources, but you know a lot about your users, so use this information. Remember that wants, needs and attitudes change over time.
4 Think about it from the audience's perspective, not from your own. We are all bombarded with advertising these days, and the prospective consumer of your publicity will be asking, 'What's in it for me?' before making the decision as to whether even to look at it. People do not want management books: they want to be able to manage well, without any effort, so tell them that your management books will achieve this for them. This is known in the trade as benefit selling.
5 Tell your audience why they should obtain what they want from you rather than elsewhere. The unique selling point of libraries is that the majority of their services are offered without charge, but there is a tendency in our society only to value that which is paid for, so you might

be better advised to take the line, 'You've paid for it (via taxation) so use it'.

6 Keep it short and simple and avoid jargon. Try it out on some prospective customers (not colleagues) before going ahead – you are too close to it to see the faults.

7 Instigate a programme of press releases. Coverage by your local newspapers and magazines is free, so you need to make the most of this form of promotion, and sending out press releases is very simple now that you can fax or e-mail to multiple destinations at the touch of a button. The media are always eager for things to print, but it must be news, not announcements. You will not have your press release used if you say that you have an excellent health information section; you will if you say that Joe Bloggs had his life changed by the information he was given, and a quote from Joe is even better. If there is not any obvious news, make some – be the first to do something, or the biggest, or record your thousandth customer, or tell them how Mrs Bloggs had a sentimental reunion with her sister in Australia via your e-mail facilities. Once you start looking for news it is plentiful: you only have to develop the right frame of mind. Once you've got your 'spin', write your release, putting the main facts in the first paragraph, and adding less crucial details as you go on: if they are short of space they will cut from the bottom up. After the text, give a contact name for editors to use if they require more information. Find out which reporters cover your sector (local government, education or whatever) for your local paper, and develop a relationship with them: they can be very helpful.

8 Don't be afraid of media like radio and television. Local radio stations, like local papers, are always crying out for people who will talk to them about something interesting. They are not going to try and trip you up, they want to help you, and most broadcasts are recorded so if you get in a tangle it can be done again. Go on a course to learn to do it: the first time's the worst and much easier in a pretend situation.

9 Remember to use your website to gain publicity.

Reading development

Reading development is a term which applies primarily to public libraries, and is a phrase which sums up the concept of not just buying popular stock, or just buying stock and putting it on the shelves for people to find if they happen to look. It is about selecting a wide range of stock which will allow people to stretch, enrich and enjoy themselves, and about promoting the stock so customers are led to it, and are led to try different areas of reading. It starts with enabling people – young or otherwise – to develop their functional literacy, which is so important in every area of life. Beyond that, it is aimed at stimulating interest in reading by such means as:

- book displays
- promotions
- author events
- readers (and writers) in residence
- reading groups
- websites allowing readers to interact with each other as well as the library
- having trained staff able to guide and prompt individuals according to their reading needs.

Librarians have been undertaking reading development for many years, but the term is one with a much higher profile in the last couple of years. Part of the ICT training for staff recommended by the UK's Library and Information Commission in *Building the New Library Network* (1998) is to do with reading development and aims to ensure that staff:

- are aware of reader-related sites on the internet, including
  — thematic approaches and guides to further reading
  — sites on specific genres and authors
  — online bookstores
  — publishers' sites
  — reading groups
- know about literacy initiatives in education, such as the national literacy strategy
- know about Bookstart and other early-reading initiatives, and have a working knowledge of sites for children and their reading
- know about sites and sources of interest to readers with a range of special needs.

When looking to develop promotions, displays and suchlike, it is obviously sensible for libraries to work together to save each inventing the same wheel. One initiative of particular note in this field is Branching Out, which is managed by a firm called Opening the Book Ltd, and which receives national lottery money via the Arts Council of England to develop various reader development projects which library authorities can then buy into. They will do different things for different projects, but all will have a book list of titles relevant to the theme, some ideas to help bring the promotion alive, ready-made training sessions for staff and press release texts. Examples of the projects include:

- 'Get Lost', a promotion highlighting books that put the reader into a different world: a mixture of imaginative fiction and non-fiction.
- 'Get a Grip', a promotion featuring books from a wide range of genres: crime, thrillers and horror but also including a range of non-fiction titles, short stories, Black and Asian writing and literature from around the world.
- 'Get a Life', a promotion which explores other people's lives through diaries, letters, biographies, scandals and lies.

Children's reading

The UK government has recently provided funding towards 'joined-up reading support' for children, using schools and public libraries.

In 2004 the Department for Education and Skills (DfES) helped fund the Summer Reading Challenge run by public libraries, and more recently the same department has funded a pack called *Enjoying Reading and Developing Reading Communities*. This is designed to assist public library staff in building partnerships with schools. It outlines the policy for the joined-up approach and helps by listing key research and case studies.

Another national initiative that can be described as reading development, although it is also highly effective in the areas of lifelong learning and social inclusion, is Bookstart. This is an initiative that gives a book-bag, with books, information on reading with your child and library joining forms, to every child in an area when it is eight months old: the scheme works in conjunction with health visitors, who see all children at this age for a hearing test. The idea started in Birmingham, but large-scale initial sponsorship from Sainsbury's for several years enabled it to spread to most of the UK and it is being funded currently by the DfES. A research project by Birmingham University has studied the effects of the initiative, and has proved beyond doubt that Bookstart babies when they reach school age are ahead of their peers in both literacy and numeracy. The scheme has its effect on the rest of the family, too, with many showing an increase in their use of books, in the sharing of books between family members and in their use of libraries.

Another similar but wider initiative is now underway, led by government and called Sure Start, in which many libraries have become involved.

The wider context in the UK

It should be obvious from this chapter so far that libraries have been altered in many ways over the last decade, and have seen huge changes over recent years. Public library services in particular, which were previously responsible mainly to their local authority, are now far more influenced by central government and other national influences. Many of these influences have been cited above, but a mention must be made of some others to complete the picture.

The People's Network and the impact of ICT on the future role of libraries

The most influential documents of the 1990s for public libraries were two written by the Library and Information Commission (LIC): *New Library: the People's Network* in 1997 and *Building the New Library Network* in 1998. They were primarily about the provision of ICT, but also helped to clarify the role of the modern public library generally (LIC, 1997; 1998).

The basic concept of the People's Network has ensured all public libraries have computers for public use linked to the internet and to the National Grid for Learning (NGfL). It also ensured that all public library staff were trained in the ICT skills that their particular job demanded. The LIC's clarity of vision and skilled analysis of the use of ICT in libraries doubtless did much to ensure that the case put forward was accepted by the government, and millions of pounds were made available to achieve it via the New Opportunities Fund of the lottery.

Data are published on the MLA website that indicate its impact and the changes in public libraries that have ensued (www.mla.gov.uk/action/pn/fastfacts.asp):

- There are more than 4000 public libraries across the UK offering free or low cost broadband internet access and other services.
- Over 30,000 computer terminals with broadband internet access provide over 68.5 million hours of internet use every year across the UK.
- There are 3500 public libraries in England offering more than 20,000 computer terminals.

- Many libraries provide access to assistive technology to help people who find conventional computer facilities difficult to use.
- More than 40,000 public library staff are trained to use computers and assist the public in their online and information needs.

Shortly after the People's Network was formally launched survey data revealed that:

- 27% of People's Network users had never used the internet before.
- In the first few months of the service 25,000 people had started a new course or gained a qualification online.
- 8,000 users had found new jobs by using the People's Network.
- 52,000 people have used the service for activities supporting their local community.

Librarians need to embrace this new method of storage and communication. It is already worrying to see many large firms creating 'knowledge management' posts and not recognizing that librarians are the people with the skills to fill them. Library staff are becoming increasingly valuable employees as they add ICT skills to their existing people skills and organization of information skills; whether the pay the job receives will come to reflect this remains to be seen.

The way in which the library service is offered to the public also needs to undergo a fundamental overhaul. The idea of having a repository of information and learning materials in a certain place available only at certain times does not fit our society today, with its emphasis on instant, constant and easy access. In their information and learning roles, libraries are moving towards becoming online gateways, able to provide up-to-date, accurate, validated and comprehensive signposts to the material required by the user at any time and from any place. See www.webrary.org for an example of how an American library is approaching this. Their site includes:

- booklists arranged by the type of characters involved (e.g. 'manly men doing manly things manfully') or by genre (e.g. 'seriously humorous mysteries')
- new title information; readers can key in their areas of interest (both fiction and non-fiction) and see a monthly list of additions to the library's stock in these areas
- support material for the library's regular book group

- an online book club, which provides extracts from best-selling books each day by e-mail, to tempt people into reserving the titles and reading them in full.

At the moment, the people mentioned under the last bullet point have to go to their local library to get the book, but in the future they could be downloading the title from the library site.

ICT is bringing huge opportunities to libraries; it also carries huge threats. There are competitors in nearly every area of service who are rapidly exploiting the internet. Unless public libraries change rapidly and appropriately they are under threat, and there is not a single member of staff who does not need to take this on board and recognize their role in the change. The change will not go away, and cannot be ignored out of concern for current users' needs, which may be seen as not served by the changes. The challenge is to keep current users happy while becoming relevant to those who do not use libraries, especially the young, who may otherwise grow up with no concept of the relevance of libraries to their lives.

The coming of ICT and of the 24/7 society (which demands services be available 24 hours a day, seven days a week) is leading to a need to rebalance the spending of library budgets. Hardware and software is expensive, and becomes obsolete quickly, and the staff time needed to create a virtual library or to support users on PCs is considerable. Within any given service the challenge is a difficult one, but one option being developed in both the public and the academic sectors is self-service: people are used to self-service at petrol stations and banks, and often prefer it. All circulation systems have developed or are developing self-issue and return facilities, which can be linked to a book security system if desired. The library authority in Trafford has even been trying out the concept of allowing access to a library at times when it is not staffed, controlled by use of a smartcard.

Developing the first phase of the People's Network Service

As stated on the MLA website (www.mla.gov.uk/action/pn/services.asp), 'The vision of the People's Network Service is to create an innovative web-based resource which complements and builds on the core strengths of public libraries; bringing easy access to information, inspiration and learning opportunities to an expanding community of users.' To this end the MLA, supported by a £500,000 grant from the Big Lottery Fund, is developing the first phase of the People's Network Service during 2004–2005. The work will be divided into two strands: the online services and the range of accessible resources.

The online services

- enquiry: a 24-hour, seven-days-a-week, real-time online enquiry service
- discovery: a place for people to find resources of relevance to their particular needs
- reading: online reading groups for adults and other services to support reading development.

The resources

- cultural resources to inform and promote a sense of place
- community information resources to highlight local activities
- reference resources to support knowledge and understanding
- government resources to aid active citizenship
- learning resources to assist informal and formal learning.

Government influence and national initiatives

As indicated above, the effect of government policies on libraries is much greater than ever before, both directly and indirectly – libraries are being affected not just by library policies, but by policies to do with areas such as lifelong learning and social inclusion. Three examples are given below.

1 The academic sector – universities, colleges and schools – has seen big changes in funding arrangements, which have altered their degree of autonomy and how they are controlled, and have made them more competitive. Students now pay tuition fees, the percentage of mature students is increasing and learning is increasingly demanded at a time and a place suited to the student, not the institution. All this is having its effect on academic libraries. There is a demand for much longer opening hours (helping to drive the implementation of self-service) and students are becoming more demanding as they use their own money to pay for their education.

2 Health information libraries may also find themselves affected by government changes – to the National Health Service in this case – notably the provision of NHS Direct, where advice and information can be

obtained from a national phone line. All callers may be offered further information about their problem; this information has to be supplied from somewhere, and the task is a large one. Existing services may be used, and health librarians will certainly be needed; each area of the country is coming up with its own ways of organizing this.

3 Public libraries are being affected by, among other things, fundamental changes being made in the education sector. The government is reorganizing not only teaching itself, but support services such as the provision of information, advice and guidance (IAG). IAG is about helping individuals to decide what they want to do, what education or training is needed to achieve it and how this education or training can be obtained. The service offered to adults is called IAG, while the one for young people has been given the brand name Connexions. Both are seen not so much as services in their own right, but as organizations to help pull together a lot of existing provision and make it more effective. To this end they are asking bodies like public libraries to become accredited partners, which means the library service has to undergo an accreditation process in order to receive the IAG branding. The idea is an excellent one, but the accreditation process can be onerous, especially if multiple organizations (the Community Legal Service is another, for example) require different accreditation processes: a little more 'joined-up thinking' is required to reduce this load. The other area where public libraries have to exercise some caution is in ensuring that their ethics and ethos are not undermined in the process. In the IAG world, for example, it is seen as desirable to track the next steps of someone who uses the services to assess its effectiveness, but public libraries do not require their customers to identify themselves and would not wish to do so.

Partnerships

Finally, it cannot be emphasized enough that the way forward for libraries lies in partnerships. Partnerships have many advantages. They can:

- bring together complementary agencies to create a whole which is more than the sum of the parts
- achieve very cost-effective services
- help avoid duplication of effort and 'wheels being reinvented'
- avoid duplication of services or identify gaps
- allow people with various fields of expertise to contribute and interact.

Partnerships for libraries may be with:

- other libraries in a geographical area
- libraries from other sectors
- other agencies
- the voluntary sector
- the business sector.

Geographical partnerships may come together for purely internal reasons, such as stock-purchasing consortia aiming to negotiate better discounts with suppliers.

Partnerships of public and academic libraries in an area already exist, such as LASH: the Libraries Access Sunderland scHeme. This offers the residents of Sunderland access to every library in the city, enabling them to make use of various collections, ICT provision and the 3500 study spaces that are available. The individual libraries involved still have their own restrictions and regulations in place, but barriers have been reduced to a minimum, and a website (www.lash.sunderland.ac.uk) gives details of the opening hours and facilities of each library.

Joint public/school libraries are another possibility, ensuring better use of the school stocks, a wider range of stock available to the pupils, and input of expertise from both sectors. These exist in many authorities and are organized in varying ways, with differing reports as to their level of success.

Many other agencies already have a partnership with libraries, possibly in the form of using library space once a month to give their service a higher profile and make it more accessible to the public. Examples include the Benefits Agency and the Inland Revenue. Greater integration of ser-vices is coming about, as explained above, with agencies who have shared objectives with the library service, such as the IAG partnerships and the Community Legal Service. The partnership with health visitors has been crucial to the success of the Bookstart initiative.

Partnerships with the voluntary sector are already widely in existence, though it is likely they will be substantially increased, given the necessity of using voluntary organizations to help achieve social inclusion and the likely increasing use of volunteers to help run aspects of the service. Many public libraries use organizations like the WRVS to help deliver books to housebound people – a partnership that has worked well for many years.

Links with the business sector, other than through sponsorship, are currently less common, though again are likely to increase. One route this could take is for businesses to give libraries the ability to provide a loan service in a place convenient to the user: Ford in Dagenham, for example, enabled books to be brought into their factory from the local library to be borrowed by their employees. The government's report *Culture and Creativity: the next ten years* (DCMS, 2001) suggests extending rural library provision by having book collections and computer terminals in post offices.

What matters is fulfilling the needs of the community, not the way in which this is done or by whom, and the government is making it clear that it will not allow any government body to be precious about its services. Libraries of all types offer a superb service, but public libraries in particular need to change to keep up with technological and cultural changes in society. They have the ability to do so, and the UK library service of 2020 is one to be looked forward to with eager anticipation.

References

Brighton's New Jubilee Library (2005) Brighton's New Jubilee Library, *Library and Information Update*, **4** (1–2), January/February, 5.

CoLRiC (n.d.) Council for Learning Resources in Colleges, *Guidelines for Self-assessment of College Learning Resources Services*, Blackburn, CoLRiC.

Department of Culture, Media and Sport (2001) Great Britain, Department of Culture, Media and Sport, *Culture and Creativity: the next ten years*, London, DCMS.

Department of the Environment, Transport and the Regions (1998) Great Britain, Department of the Environment, Transport and the Regions, White Paper: *Modernising Local Government: improving local services through best value*, London, DETR.

Eynon, A. (ed.) (2005) *Guidelines for Colleges: recommendations for learning resources*, London, Facet Publishing.

Framework for the Future (2003) Department for Culture, Media and Sport, *Framework for the Future: libraries, learning and information in the next decade*, London, DCMS, www.culture.gov.uk/global/publications/archive_2003/framework_future. htm.

Library and Information Commission (1998) *Building the New Library Network: a report to the Government*, London, LIC.

Library and Information Commission (1997) *New Library: the People's Network*, London, LIC, www.ukoln.ac.uk/services/lic/newlibrary.

Appendix to Chapter 7: Health and Safety at Work etc. Act 1974

The Health and Safety at Work etc. Act 1974 is the principal piece of health and safety legislation in this country. Prior to the 1974 Act, health and safety laws were complex and left a significant proportion of the workforce unprotected. Some previous legislation (e.g. Factories Act 1961, Offices, Shops and Railway Premises Act 1963) may still apply to certain premises or activities.

The Health and Safety at Work Act:

* provides one comprehensive and integrated system of law dealing with health, safety and welfare arising out of work activities
* imposes general duties for health and safety at work
* covers everyone at work who may be affected by work activities
* established the Health and Safety Commission and the Health and Safety Executive
* provides the legal framework for further health and safety legislation.

Under the 1974 Act, both employers and employees have duties, although the bulk of the responsibility rests with the employer.

Employers' duties are to:

* ensure, so far as is reasonably practicable, the health, safety and welfare of all employees and any other people who may use their premises or be affected by their business
* provide a written policy statement explaining how they intend to do this
* provide appropriate training, instruction, supervision and information.

Employees' duties are to:

* co-operate with employers' arrangements for ensuring health and safety
* take reasonable care of the health and safety of themselves and others.

The 1974 Act gives only general guidance about health and safety. Since the 1974 Act, several regulations have been passed which give more detail about particular situations (e.g. The Control of Substances Hazardous to Health Regulations 1988, The Management of Health and Safety at Work

Regulations 1992). Some of these regulations have been introduced to bring UK health and safety law into line with European laws.

Other official documents include Approved Codes of Practice and Guidance Notes. These are intended to give practical guidance for complying with regulations but are not an authoritative interpretation of the law. Failure to comply with the ACoP will not per se render liability to criminal or civil proceedings: however, following guidance will usually be sufficient to comply with the law.

Summary

- The Health and Safety at Work Act 1974 is the fundamental piece of health and safety legislation in this country.
- It covers everyone who is affected by work activity.
- It is a general document, which places the burden of legal responsibility for health and safety at work with the employer.
- Regulations made under the Act give much more detailed legal requirements.
- Approved Codes of Practice and Guidance Notes give information about how to comply with health and safety law.

References

Health and Safety Commission (1992) *Management of Health and Safety at Work: management of Health and Safety at Work regulations 1992: approved code of practice*, London, HMSO, 1992.

Health and Safety Commission (1994) *The Protection of Persons Against Ionising Radiation Arising from any Activity*, London, HSE Books.

Health and Safety Executive (2005) *Control of Substances Hazardous to Health, and The Control of Substances Hazardous to Health Regulations 2002 as amended: approved code of practice and guidance*, Sudbury, HSE Books.

Health and Safety Executive (2000) *Essentials of Health and Safety at Work*, London, HSE Executive.

USDAW (n.d.) *Health and Safety Reps Handbook*, USDAW (Union of Shop, Distributive and Allied Workers), latest edition continually available at www.usdaw.org.uk/getactive/resource_library/1058882019_2714.html.

8 The international perspective

International organizations which support libraries

IFLA (www.ifla.org/III/index.htm)

IFLA, the International Federation of Library Associations and Institutions, represents the interests of library and information services across the world. It has been described as the global voice of the library and information profession. IFLA's core functions are emphasized in its recently introduced model: the Society Pillar deals with the role and impact of library and information services on society, the Profession Pillar focuses on professional practice and the Members Pillar focuses on members, conferences and publications. IFLA has regional offices in Africa, Asia and Oceania and Latin America. Electronic communication is handled by IFLANET. We must also mention in this context the World Summit on the Information Society held in October 2004, where 99 delegates from 18 countries discussed the problems of libraries in the information society and in which IFLA was heavily involved.

UNESCO (http://portal.unesco.org/ci/en/ev.php)

For the last 60 years UNESCO has promoted the work of libraries globally, concentrating on, for example, standards for national libraries, the development of information technology, particularly in the least developed countries, and on libraries as a tool of education. To quote the UNESCO website, 'Libraries are essential to the free flow of ideas and to maintaining, increasing and spreading knowledge. As repositories of books and other printed material, they are the key to promoting reading and writing.'

It was a great relief to the British library sector when Britain rejoined UNESCO when a Labour government was elected in 1997.

Book Aid International (www.bookaid.org/cms.cgi/site/about/)

Book Aid International is the major charity dealing with the provision of books to less developed countries. Its slogan is 'Opening up the world through books'.

'If education is the road out of poverty, books are the wheels needed for the journey' (Richard Crabbe, Chairman, Africa Publishers Network, 1997–2002). Formerly the Ranfurly Library Service, Book Aid International targets those areas in greatest need of books for all readers, at the same time encouraging the development of appropriate technology. BAI works in partnership with local bodies and with organizations such as Voluntary Service Overseas and the British Council. There is an emphasis on sub-Saharan Africa (see the case study below).

We must also note the advocacy role of Book Aid International – it submitted evidence to Tony Blair's Commission for Africa and to the Make Poverty History Campaign.

It is heartening to note that following the Asian tsunami disaster of December 2004 all three of these international organizations are closely involved in helping to rebuild the many libraries devastated by the flooding, as is CILIP, which has an International Officer. It would certainly seem there is indeed a global and co-operative perspective in the library and information sector today which is greatly to be commended.

Libraries in the developed world
General

We had intended originally to offer in this section an overview of library provision in the developed world, but this has proved extremely difficult to research in any meaningful way. We have therefore provided a case study from Western Australia to illustrate typical provision.

In the developed world there is a largely common pattern of provision. There is a national library – for example, the Bibliothèque Nationale in France and the National Library of Australia. There are networks of public library services involving books, newspapers and magazines, a reference service, internet access and provision for minority groups as part of social inclusion efforts. Services are usually available to everyone in the catchment area and are normally entirely or partially free. Funding is usually through state and local government. There are usually recognized degree-level qualifications for professional library staff. It has been suggested that the status of library and information staff is higher in some countries, such as Australia, New Zealand and the USA, than it is in the UK.

Case study: Western Australia (www.liswa.wa.gov.au/publibs.html)

To quote from the website:

Public libraries in Western Australia offer a wide range of resources and services for everybody. These can include:-

* Books for recreation and information for people of all ages
* Newspapers and magazines
* Reference sources including encyclopaedias and directories
* Large print books
* Videos including some with captions
* CD-ROMs, computing and internet facilities
* Music cassettes, CDs, games and jigsaws
* Books and other resources in 50 community languages other than English
* Resources for learning a language and language learning resource centres
* Community and local history information
* Photocopying facilities.

Public libraries also provide:

* Resources and services for children and young people
* Services for seniors
* Services for a multicultural Western Australia
* Services for Aboriginal and Torres Strait islanders
* Assistance with literacy and numeracy
* Services to people with disabilities

You are entitled to join your local public library in the area in which you live, work, or go to school. All you will be required to do is show identification and proof of your current address. There is no charge for joining your local library.

We also learn that libraries in Western Australia are provided by a partnership between state and local government.

With a few details changed, much of the above could apply to thousands of public libraries across the UK, the rest of Europe, parts of Asia, the USA, Australia, New Zealand and Canada. The provision of a robust public library system is clearly essential to a successful and contented country.

We should also mention the importance of the great libraries attached to academic institutes throughout the world.

Libraries in the developing world

We decided to include coverage of libraries in the developing world for a number of reasons. There is a current focus through the Make Poverty History campaign (see below) on the ways in which a less inequitable world can be created, and the importance of educational resources in that fight.

During the writing of this book we have found a great contrast between the pessimism of some current attitudes to library provision in the West, for example the recent suggestion by the Chairman of Waterstone's that public libraries in this country will have died out within 15 years, and the idealism, enthusiasm and confidence in the vital importance of library resources which characterizes the outlook of practitioners in the developing world.

The ethical dimension of the profession is strengthened by global co-operation and the desire to extend to all the social, educational and cultural benefits of a comprehensive and flexible library and information system as part of the route out of poverty and deprivation.

General

The developed world is at last focusing on the needs of the developing world. Poverty, climate change, war, corrupt governments, disease, unfair trading conditions, poor educational resources and natural disasters have contributed to a very inequitable global picture.

The Make Poverty History campaign and similar initiatives are currently focusing on these injustices. With education being a major route out of poverty, and books and information technology being a major resource in education, it is heartening to see the very real strides being made by the work of Book Aid International in providing, in partnership with local organizations, some of the tools needed for progress.

Case study: sub-Saharan Africa

Book Aid International's strategy is to put books into the hands of the world's most disadvantaged readers.

Working in 18 countries in sub-Saharan Africa and Palestine, BAI provides over 500,000 books and journals annually to libraries, hospitals, refugee camps and schools. These books are donated by UK publishers, libraries, schools and individual donors, and can be fiction and non-fiction for children and adults as well as professional and educational material. Books should not be more than 10 years old and in good condition. Most are obviously in English, which is often the language used for educational purposes, particularly in areas where tribal languages have an oral rather than a written tradition, but Book Aid International also purchases books directly from publishers in the UK and in Africa and gives grants to partner libraries in Africa to buy books locally in local languages.

As well as the provision of books and other resources Book Aid International is involved in training, skills sharing and advocacy.

To quote from the Book Aid website:

> Books are the basic tools of literacy and education yet millions of children and adults in the developing world do not have access to them.

> Books can make a real difference to people's lives. Farmers, nurses, mechanics, development workers and teachers all need books and information to support their work. Children and students must be encouraged to use books to develop their education and lifelong learning.

> The majority of our support goes to rural and urban libraries which are free and accessible to everyone. Book Aid International works with library partners to develop their pivotal role in the community.

Conclusion

In the developed world we tend to take good library provision for granted, and perhaps not value it as the vital component in a successful society that it clearly is. A study of libraries in the developing world provides a salutary reminder that we should work to maintain the excellent provision most of us enjoy, and we should endeavour to ensure that the developing world can soon begin to share in our good fortune.

Useful sources of information

Books

Beecroft, K. A. (ed.) *CILIP Yearbook*, London, Facet Publishing, annual.

Chowdhury, G. G. and Chowdhury, S. (2001) *Searching CD-ROM and Online Information Sources*, London, Library Association Publishing (now Facet Publishing).

Duckett, B., Walker, P. and Donnelly, C. (2004) *Know it All, Find it Fast*, rev. edn, London, Library Association Publishing (now Facet Publishing).

Owen, T. (2003) *Success at the Enquiry Desk*, 4th edn, London, Library Association Publishing (now Facet Publishing).

Poulter, A., Hiom, D. and McMenemy, D. (2005) *The Library and Information Professional's Internet Companion*, London, Facet Publishing.

School Library Association (regular updates) *Guidelines*, Swindon, SLA.

For those interested in college libraries, CoLRiC (Council for Learning Resources in Colleges) and COHFE (Colleges of Higher and Further Education Group of CILIP) respectively issue guidelines for the inspection of college libraries, and guidelines for the performance and resourcing of college libraries. Current editions are:

CoLRiC (n.d.) Council for Learning Resources in Colleges, *Guidelines for Self-assessment of College Learning Resources Services*, Blackburn, CoLRiC.

Eynon, A. (ed.) (2005) *Guidelines for Colleges: recommendations for learning resources*, London, Facet Publishing.

There have also been over the last few years a number of relevant central government publications, reflecting the major initiatives which have been introduced, for example:

Department for Culture, Media and Sport (2003) *Framework for the Future*, London, DCMS.
Department for Culture, Media and Sport (2004) *Public Library Matters*, London, DCMS.

Journals

A variety of relevant publications in the library and information field can be useful and interesting for the paraprofessional. We particularly recommend close reading of the CILIP *Library and Information Update* (monthly) and the CILIP *Gazette* (fortnightly) for current information about the sector. We also recommend the *School Librarian*, published quarterly by the School Library Association.

Websites

Audit Commission: www.audit-commission.gov.uk
British Library: www.bl.uk
CILIP: www.cilip.org.uk
Department for Culture, Media and Sport: www.culture.gov.uk
Learndirect: www.learndirect.co.uk
Lifelong Learning: www.lifelonglearning.co.uk
Museums Libraries and Archives Council: www.mla.gov.uk
National Grid for Learning: www.ngfl.gov.uk
People's Network: www.peoplesnetwork.gov.uk

Glossary of abbreviations and acronyms

AACR2	*Anglo-American Cataloguing Rules*, 2nd edn
ADSL	Asymmetric digital subscriber line
ARLIS	Art Libraries Society
ARTTel	Automated Request Transmission by Telecommunications
Aslib	Association of Special Libraries and Information Bureaux (Association for Information Management)
ASSIA	*Applied Social Science Index and Abstracts*
BAI	Book Aid International (formerly Ranfurly Library Service)
BL	British Library
BLDSC	British Library Document Supply Service
BNB	British National Bibliography
BSI	British Standards Institution
CAB	Citizens Advice Bureaux
CD-ROM	Compact disc read-only memory
CEEFAX	Teletext service provided in the UK by the BBC
CGLI	City and Guilds of London Institute
CILIP	Chartered Institute of Library and Information Professionals
CIPFA	Chartered Institute of Public Finance and Accountancy
CLS	Community Legal Service
CMF	Capital Modernization Fund
CoLRiC	Council for Learning Resources in Colleges

CONARLS	Circle of Officers of National and Regional Library Systems
DCMS	Department for Culture, Media and Sport
DTP	Desktop publishing
ECCTIS	Education Counselling and Credit Transfer Information Service
ERASMUS	European Community Action Scheme for the Mobility of University Students
EU	European Union
fax	facsimile transmission
FTP	File transfer protocol
HEFC	Higher Education Funding Council
HRM	Human resources management
IAG	Information, advice and guidance
ICT	Information and communication technology
IFLA	International Federation of Library Associations and Institutions
IIP	Investors in People
ISBN	International Standard Book Number
ISDN	Integrated services digital network
ISO	International Organization for Standardization
ISP	Internet service provider
ISSN	International Standard Serial Number
IT	Information technology
JANET	Joint Academic NETwork
LA	Library assistant
LAN	Local area network
LC	Library of Congress
LINC	Library and Information Co-operation Council
LISA	*Library and Information Science Abstracts*
LSC	Learning and Skills Council
MARC	MAchine Readable Cataloguing
MCI	Management Charter Initiative
NOF	New Opportunities Fund
NVQ	National Vocational Qualification
OPAC	Online public access catalogue
PC	Personal computer
PI	Performance indicator
PLUS	Public Library User Survey
QAA	Quality Assurance Agency

SCONUL	Society of College, National and University Libraries
SLA	School Library Association
SWRLS	South Western Regional Library System
TIC	Tourist Information Centre
UDC	Universal Decimal Classification
VDU	Visual display unit
WAN	Wide area network
WP	Word processor
WWW	world wide web

Index